Pure and Simple

Delicious Whole Natural Foods Cookbook
Vegan, MSG Free and Gluten Free
By Tami A. Benton

foodasgrown.

To order more cookbooks go to

foodasgrown.com

Use your own judgment: We made these recipes to *our* level of tolerance for MSG and gluten which seems to greatly benefit the majority of people, but may not be right for everyone. *Use your own judgment for your own health condition.* Also, in consideration of such a wide range of people enjoying these recipes, in a few cases we have left the wheat option there along with the gluten free option, so everyone can choose.

MSG-sensitive individuals: Long cooking times at high heat may cause problems for *extremely* sensitive individuals. In addition, tomatoes, corn and soy contain small amounts of free glutamic acid. For most people these foods are healthful and safe. See msgmyth.com for more information about MSG.

Celiac individuals: Although oats are gluten free, they may be grown with trace amounts of wheat. In addition some who react to gluten also react to the protein in oats. Extremely sensitive individuals may want to avoid the few recipes that use oats or use safer oats, such as those from glutenfreeoats.com or creamhillestates.com

ISBN: 978-0-9796443-0-6

foodasgrown.com

You're Gonna Love it!

This book is designed to help those who would like to add delicious, whole foods to their diet. In addition, it will assist those who wish to reduce or avoid wheat, gluten, MSG, dairy, eggs, animal foods, sulfites and yeast.

My husband and I have to avoid allergens and MSG, but we still *love* flavor. My husband had felt deprived of tasty food until I started cooking for him. It was a big challenge, greatly modifying nearly every recipe I found. My solution was to start with natural foods and use more herbs for flavor rather than MSG. The result was very satisfying. Now we've found that many people want tasty, whole foods and a healthier life.

So these recipes are for you, hoping that your journey to health is both delightful and a little easier.

> *These recipes are so delicious that I can take them to any group of people and get positive comments on the flavor. Even people eating the typical American diet have asked for recipes.*

foodasgrown.com

3

Acknowledgments

Special thanks to my husband Gary for the encouragement he has given me, for tasting the food and giving feedback, and for the countless hours he spent helping me put the recipes in this cookbook. His experience working in print shops was key in preparing the book for publication.

Thanks to my mom, for allowing the kitchen to be an environment, where even as a young child, I could come in, pull up a chair, and stir the batter.

Thanks to Toni Busby for giving helpful advice and encouragement, to Debbie Forsyth for her belief in the project, and to many other friends and family who showed support. Thanks to the many children who eagerly ate the smoothies and muffins and asked for more.

Note from Gary: Thanks to Tami for figuring out how to make delicious food despite having to avoid MSG, wheat, dairy, and even beans for a time. The years of trying to adapt recipes, learning to season food to create sensational flavors merits my highest praise. Her creativity in designing the cover amazed me, and she deserves full credit for a fantastic job on it.

Dedication

This book is dedicated to my husband, Gary.
You knew, you always believed, and you even helped.

Pure and Simple...

We chose this title because all the ingredients are very pure, without additives, sugar, artificial flavors and colors, or MSG. We purchase most of the items in the produce section and the bulk foods aisle of the store. We use mostly foods as grown. The few items that come in a can have very pure, simple ingredients, often just the main item and some salt.

The recipes are not complicated and are written in a quick to use format. In some recipes, the preparation is very quick; other recipes take a little longer. It is as quick as we could make it while still using pure, natural ingredients, and the steps are still clear and easy to follow.

I like to take shortcuts, so I have simplified the steps as much as I could for each recipe. The recipes that do take a little longer are ones that are *so delicious* that I still find them worth the time when I have it.

foodasgrown.com

Table of Contents

Note: Recipes are arranged for browsing pleasure to create a feeling of choice, variety, and visual stimulation. For the times when you prefer alphabetical order, we also included an index at the back. We hope you enjoy wandering through our cookbook, gathering inspiration along the way.

Adjusting to Diet Changes

Be kind to yourself. It takes time to develop your new favorite healthy food replacements. Don't expect yourself to accomplish everything all at once. Start adding in more natural foods for now, and later you can adjust your diet as you feel the need or desire.

Be kind to me. This cookbook does not represent the perfect diet, but rather an improvement over the average diet. If your diet is stricter regarding use of packaged foods, oils, salt or anything else, that's fine, just adjust to fit your needs or skip a recipe.

Be kind to your friends and family. Whenever there are two different diets, the question comes up, "Which one is right and which one is wrong?" For fear of being wrong, your friend or relative may become defensive or appear to attack.
To ease this situation, it is very helpful to **allow *both* diets to be acceptable**. Find YOUR PERSONAL MOTIVATION for having your diet, a reason that is DIFFERENT from your friend or relative. Share it in a humble manner. Some examples:

> "I really had to start changing my diet because I felt so tired and groggy all the time."
> "I get headaches when I eat that."
> "I need to stay healthy because I am an older parent and want to be around for my kids."
> "I had high blood pressure and I HAD to change."

Your friend or relative can sympathize with your situation without feeling the pressure to change. If you are willing to be humble not haughty, you can keep your diet and your friends.

Health is a journey. Find your own motivation, and be kind.

Ingredient Notes

- All nuts in this cookbook are raw (unless otherwise noted). This makes creamier tasting recipes and increases nutrition.

- Medjool dates have such a nice, mild flavor as a sweetener, that I tend to use them nearly exclusively. One Medjool date equals 2 regular dates. Be sure to remove pits.

- TAPIOCA FLOUR: You can buy tapioca pearls, or a box of minute tapioca, and grind to a flour in a Vita-Mix.

- OAT FLOUR: Blend approximately 1 ½ C oats in blender until powdered. Oat flour can also be purchased at many grocery stores.

- Bob's Red Mill brand carries many gluten free flours, including quinoa, oat, rice, buckwheat, and many others. Safeway carries this brand as well as many grocery stores.

- SOAKING NUTS: Start with **almonds**, since they need to be soaked more often. Here's an easy plan: While putting away the groceries, dump some of the **almonds in a bowl** and **cover with water** an inch or more above the nuts. (Keep some dry for eating plain or when needing dry nuts.) Then, roughly **8 hours** or so later (like before bed, or in the morning), dump off the water, put them in a ziplock bag and freeze. Soaked almonds will be smoother in many recipes and may be more easily digested.

  Cashews and macadamia are very soft nuts, so soak them for only an hour. Other nuts can be soaked like almonds.

- OUT OF SOAKED NUTS: You can use a smaller amount of non-soaked nuts when you are out of soaked nuts.

- Vanilla beans are approximately 6 inches long. Cut into one-inch pieces. One inch equals one teaspoon vanilla extract.

foodasgrown.com

Helpful Hints

- Need fast food? Make a smoothie!

- Once you know you like a recipe, always make extra to freeze. (Breads, pastas, and legumes freeze well. Cooked vegetables don't.)

- Make extra salad dressing and freeze it in a large ziplock bag about ½ inch thick. This way it is easy to break off a chunk and take along to a restaurant, on a trip, or toss in with your lunch.

- Nut creams and smoothies freeze well. Make and freeze the night before you will be traveling.

- Salad can be the main dish. Make it huge (see p. 46).

- You may want to experiment with having a light breakfast for more energy. (Heavy breakfasts made sense 100 years ago when farmers did *hard work* for a few *hours* before breakfast.) You could try fruit, or a smoothie. Include a few nuts as desired to make it easier to last until lunch.

- If mornings are hectic, throw your smoothie ingredients in a bag the night before and put in refrigerator. In the morning dump, blend, and run!

- Always be prepared with good food. Bring along fruit, dressings, breads, or even a main dish if needed when you go somewhere.

- *Every* meal? If I ate 2 or 3 dishes of asparagus every meal for a year, you might wonder about my diet. But if I ate 2 or 3 different types of wheat every meal for my whole life, I would be a normal American. Consider this menu. Breakfast: Raisin Bran, toast and a muffin. Lunch: sandwich, Wheat Thins, and a slice of banana bread. Supper: spaghetti and garlic bread with carrot cake for dessert. Many people can tolerate wheat. Just consider not having wheat at EVERY MEAL.

foodasgrown.com

Health Tips

After reading hundreds of health books, my husband and I have summarized many of the ideas into the following tips:

- Eat nutrient dense foods (see *Eat to Live* by Dr. Joel Fuhrman, M.D., page 49-67). Include more fruits, leafy greens and other vegetables in your diet.

- Eat something *raw* with every meal if possible.

- Reduce toxins. Fruits and vegetables contain **much** less pesticide than animal products such as dairy and meat. Animals eat pesticide-laden grass and have ten times or more the level that is in fruits and vegetables. Merely by eating more fruits and vegetables, you are **already** reducing toxins.

- Avoid MSG (monosodium glutamate). It **hides** in many ingredients, such as:

    Hydrolyzed vegetable protein, hydrolyzed anything
    Soy Sauce, Miso, Tamari Sauce, Braggs Liquid Aminos*, Nama Shoyu, etc.
    Natural flavors, natural chicken flavor, natural ___ flavor...
    Spices (often contain MSG)
    Modified food starch
    Gelatin
    Yeast extract (anything extract)
    Isolated soy protein

    See http://msgmyth.com for a list of 60 *more* ingredients containing hidden MSG.

- Craving salt? You may benefit from *ORGANIC* sodium, which is plentiful in plants like celery, and young coconut water.

- Flaxseeds, pecans, and walnuts are a good source of omega 3 fatty acids which are important. Avocados and coconuts contain good quality fats.

- Eat light, eat fresh, have fun with food!

*The company says Braggs Liquid Aminos does not contain MSG, but Gary has experienced the same ill effects that MSG causes him. If one takes soybeans and water and blends them up, they don't have the same savory taste. The process is a trade secret, but somehow they create a seasoning that tastes quite different than the original ingredients. Whether it has MSG or not, it's a processed food, and better health usually comes from natural, whole, unprocessed foods.

Need more ideas? Try these!

- Shift the balance. For 20 years, Gary ate a fairly healthy diet, but struggled with low energy, depression, and fatigue. He ate primarily grains, with some beans and a few nuts, fruits and vegetables. When he shifted the balance toward more fruits and vegetables his health improved noticeably.

- Detoxify. When your body is done digesting food, it says, "Yippee, time to clean house!" Then it starts clearing out the garbage, which can make you feel awful. Sometimes we interpret this as hunger, and we discover that it stops as soon as we eat. Give your body a little time to clean up between meals. See *Eat to Live* by Dr. Joel Fuhrman, M.D., page 164-169.

- Get the garbage OUT. When your body detoxifies, it dumps the garbage in the colon. If it doesn't get out soon, it will go back into the bloodstream, making you feel awful again. Make sure you are having regular bowel movements and that the transit time is under 24 hours. Eat beets or take charcoal and watch the stool to see how long it takes to change color. An herbal laxative may help keep things moving.

- Sensitive individuals, beware of molds and yeasts. Sun dried tomatoes may bother sensitive people because tomatoes have high moisture and less natural sugars than fruits, so molds or yeasts can develop undetectably while drying. Also if an avocado or potato has a black spot, consider throwing the whole thing out. Even if the spot is carefully cut out, Gary suffers after eating them. All these foods cause him sleepiness, low energy, brain fog, and even depression.

- Celiac disease or gluten intolerance result in an autoimmune response which flattens the villi in the small intestine, leading to malnutrition and a host of other related problems. If you are having digestive troubles or low energy, fatigue, or other unexplained chronic health conditions, you may want to explore this possibility. Gluten is found in all wheat products, as well as barley, rye, spelt, Kamut, and several other grains. White flour is also wheat.

- Still need help? We're running out of ideas, so read great books like: *The China Study*, *Eat to Live*, and *Green for Life*.

Breakfast

Tami's Granola

Top with loads of luscious blueberries, red raspberries, and bananas.

Toss the following ingredients in a large bowl:

    8 C rolled oats*
    1 C shredded coconut
    ¾ C sunflower seeds
    ¾ C almonds, chopped (soaked opt.)
    ¾ C pumpkin seeds (soaked opt.)
    ¾ C pecans, chopped

Put the following ingredients in the Vita-Mix and blend:

    ½ C maple syrup
    ½ C Medjool dates
    ½ C water
    1 whole vanilla bean (6 inches) or 2 T vanilla extract
    ½ T almond extract
    1 T flaxseed oil
    1 T liquid lecithin

Pour blended mix over the oat and nut mix and stir until everything is wet. Dehydrate for 2 to 3 days until dry at 107 degrees. Or bake at 225 for 45 min, or until dry.

Note: We like the flavor of the dehydrated version even better than the baked version, but baking is much faster. Choose the option you prefer.

*Although oats do not contain gluten, they may grow where wheat has grown and thus may contain *trace* amounts of gluten. Celiac individuals may need to avoid oats for this reason. Others who are gluten intolerant may be able to use oats, so we included this recipe.

Almond Milk

Blend in Vita-Mix or blender until smooth:

   1 C almonds, soaked (½ C before soaking)
   3 Medjool dates
   3" vanilla bean
   3 C cold water

Pour on your cereal, or drink plain.

Optional: For smoother milk, strain through nut milk bag or cheesecloth.

Note on straining: For use in recipes or for on cereal straining is not necessary. For drinking, it is a matter of personal preference. The milk will be a bit smoother and richer after straining. I tried drinking it once, after straining, and liked it so much that I sometimes take the extra time.

Another Option: Blend *just* the almonds and water. Strain. *Then* add the other ingredients and blend *again* until smooth. This retains all the date and vanilla IN the milk for nice flavor, but adds an extra step.

Cashew Pecan Milk

Blend the following in Vita-Mix or blender until very smooth:

¾ C cashews (soaked)
$^1/_8$ C Pecans
1" vanilla bean
½ banana
4 Medjool dates
3 C water (with ice cubes in it)

If using a regular blender, pour through a cheesecloth for smoother texture.

Gary's Almond Raisin Bars

A sweet treat!

Mix the following together and grind with meat grinder or Champion juicer (blank plate):

   1 C raisins
   1 C almonds (soaked...)
   1 C coconut (dried, shredded, unsulfured)
   ¼ t sea salt (Celtic sea salt is nice)
   1-2 t orange zest (finely grated orange peel), optional

Press into bars.

Variation: press into tiny thin round circles and top with a nut cream of your choice. Decorate each little cookie with a blueberry on top. CUTE! and TASTY!

Cream for Fruit

Blend in Vita-Mix or blender until smooth:

    1 C almonds, soaked
    ¼ C macadamia nuts, optional
    meat of one coconut, or ½ C other nuts (cashews, almonds, macadamias)
    2" vanilla bean or 2 t vanilla extract
    4 Medjool dates
    1 mango
    1 frozen banana
    1 C water (or enough to blend)

Serve with any fruit you like: bananas, strawberries, oranges, apples, blueberries, raspberries, pears or blackberries. Also try it over freshly blended applesauce! (See p. 23 & p. 24)

Applesauce

If you haven't tried fresh applesauce, you really must!

Chop into chunks and blend in Vita-Mix, blender, or food processor:

    2-3 apples

Fuji, Golden Delicious, Jonagold, or other apples work well. Add half a Granny Smith for a slightly tart flavor.

This recipe *begs* for *cream*! Try this or any other cream recipe. (See p. 168)

Cashew Cream

Blend in Vita-Mix or blender until smooth:

    2 C cashews, soaked for 2 hours
    4 Medjool dates
    2 inches vanilla bean
    1 ½ C cold water

If thick, add water 1 T at a time.

Gourmet Applesauce

Chop into chunks and blend in Vita-Mix, blender, or food processor. You can use the *whole apple*, peel, core and all, just take out the stem*.

    2-3 apples
    1 banana

Great just like that or top with Cashew Cream** for an elegant treat!

VARIATION 1:

    2-3 apples
    1 orange

VARIATION 2:

    2-3 apples
    1 banana
    1 orange

VARIATION 3:

    2-3 apples
    1 banana
    1 cup blueberries

VARIATION 4:

    2-3 apples
    1 banana
    1 pear

*Note: You still need to peel the oranges and bananas!
**Page 23.

Oat Waffles

Generously oil waffle iron and preheat.

Put all the ingredients in Vita-Mix or blender and blend well:

> 1 ½ C oats or ¾ C oat groats*
> ½ C soaked nuts or coconut
> 1 t salt
> 1 ½ C water

Pour into waffle iron and bake for 15 minutes.

Makes 6 small waffle squares.

Serving Suggestion: For a simple yet delicious topping, blend together a bag of frozen blueberries (about a quart) and 2 bananas.

Serving Suggestion #2: Top with a nut cream of choice for a rich tasting breakfast!

Note: If using a regular blender, do not use oat groats. They are too hard to blend smoothly.

Note 2: It's faster to use two waffle irons simultaneously if you have them.

*Some celiac individuals may need to avoid oats (see p. 2 for more information). Use Rice Pecan Waffles p. 26 for waffles without oats.

Rice Pecan Waffles

Throw all in Vita-Mix. Blend until smooth.

    1 ⅓ C uncooked brown rice*
    ⅓ C pecans
    1 ½ C water
    1 t salt
    ⅛ t nutmeg
    ¼ t anise seed
    ¼ t ginger
    ¼ t cloves

Bake in a waffle iron for 20 min. or until steam stops coming out.

*If using a regular blender, use rice flour instead of uncooked rice (you can buy bags of rice flour in health food stores). A regular blender cannot handle dry rice very well.

Oat Cakes

Emulsify together with fork:

> 1 C water
> ⅓ C oil

Add the following to oil and water and mix well:

> 2 t salt
> 1-2 T honey
> 4 C quick oats*
> ½ C rice flour
> 2 t baking powder

Spread into greased 9" x 13" pan. Bake at 375 for 15 minutes. Serve hot or cold with fruit or applesauce. Serves 4 to 6.

*See p. 2 for information about celiac disease and oats.

Oat Sausage

Savory oat side dish for breakfast or anytime.

Combine the following in a 2 quart saucepan and bring to boil:

> 1 C water
> 1 t salt
> 1 T oil
> 1 t honey
> 1 t onion powder
> ½ t sage
> 1 T yeast flakes (optional)
> ¼ t garlic powder
> ⅛ t Italian seasoning

Add oats to boiling water and simmer for 5 minutes.

> 1 C rolled oats*

Form into sausages and place on an oiled cookie sheet. Bake at 350 for 30 minutes. Turn over half way through.

*See p. 2 for information about celiac disease and oats.

Peachy Cream

Blend the following in Vita-Mix:

>2 C almonds (soaked)
>2" vanilla bean
>4 Medjool dates
>water and/or orange juice (fresh squeezed) enough to blend

Then add:

>1 banana (preferably frozen)
>1-2 C frozen peaches

Blend until smooth. Fantastic just as is! Serve in bowls or goblets.

Variation: Try this on waffles! (See p. 26 & 25)

Smoothies

Mango Smoothie

A delicious, pudding-like treat! It has an amazing, jelly-like texture!

Refrigerate ripe mangoes until cold. Peel and blend until smooth.

    2-5 mangoes

Serve in a fancy glass or goblet and eat with a spoon.

Note: Don't forget to take out the seed! The pit is very fibrous and the smoothie will not be good if you forget. (Yes, we actually had that happen!)

Durian Smoothie

Durian lovers may want a cup or more of this in one sitting. Durian texture and flavor can vary from one end of a piece to the other. Blending it evens it out so it is all sweet and smooth.

    1 lb. frozen durian

Unwrap the package of frozen durian (pitted, meat only). Blend until smooth in Vita-Mix. (This will not work in a conventional blender.)

Note: Durian may be purchased frozen in Asian food stores. It's a unique fruit with a custard-like, banana-like consistency and a sweet/savory taste. The smell can be hard to ignore, but a taste for durian can be acquired after eating it a few times. For those new to durian, a cherry-sized dollop is a good introduction. If you love durian, the flavor will draw you and nothing can come close to replacing it. Durian is "the King of Fruits".

Cranberry Smoothie

Try this for a new treat!

    12 oz cranberries (get them fresh in winter and freeze for summer)
    6 oz coconut meat
    5 Medjool dates
    2 frozen bananas
    1 inch vanilla bean (or 1 t vanilla extract)
    1 C water (adjust as needed)

Blend in Vita-Mix until smooth.

Blueberry Smoothie

Blend in Vita-Mix or blender until smooth*:

    3 C frozen blueberries
    1 banana, frozen if possible
    3" vanilla bean
    ¼ C raisins
    1 apple, peach, nectarine or equivalent amount of fresh pineapple (watery fruit
        makes blending easier) OR 1 C fruit juice (watermelon, apple, orange,
        pineapple, grape)
    water, small amount if necessary for blending

Serve in goblets.

*May need to do a half batch and add extra water if using a regular blender.

Raspberry Smoothie

Blend the following until smooth:

    3-4 C raspberries, frozen or fresh
    1 banana, frozen or fresh
    4 Medjool dates
    1 C soaked almonds (½ C if unsoaked)
    1 T vanilla extract or 3" vanilla bean
    1 juicy fruit (see below)*

Serve with frozen raspberries or blueberries and sliced banana. Nut cream makes a nice layer.

*Choose one of the following for a juicy fruit to add liquid to make the blending easier:
    1 apple
    1 orange
    1 peach
    1 nectarine
    1 – 1 ½ C fresh pineapple
    1 C fruit juice (watermelon, apple, orange, pineapple, grape).

Peach Strawberry Smoothie

1 banana, frozen or fresh
3 Medjool dates
⅓ C cashews, soaked or unsoaked
1 ½ – 2 C strawberries, frozen
1 ½ – 2 C peaches, frozen
½ C water (more for regular blender)
2 T flax oil (optional for omega 3 essential fatty acids)

Blend in Vita-Mix or blender until smooth. Serve immediately.

Blueberry Peach Smoothie

A rich, smooth treat!

Blend the following in Vita-Mix or blender until smooth:

 1 C almonds, soaked
 4 Medjool dates
 1 ½ inch vanilla bean
 1 apple (cut into several pieces)
 ½ C water

Then add the following and blend again:

 1 frozen banana
 1-2 C blueberries, frozen
 1-2 C peaches, frozen

Makes a delicious breakfast or supper for two, or a tasty dessert for 4-6.

Strawberry "Yogurt"

1 C almonds (soaked)
1 ½ inch vanilla bean (or 1 ½ t pure vanilla extract)
1 apple (cut into several pieces)
1 frozen banana
1-2 C strawberries, frozen
1-2 C peaches, frozen
½ C water

Blend in Vita-Mix or blender until smooth.

Pecan Blueberry Smoothie

A delightfully creamy, pudding-like texture!

Blend in Vita-Mix or blender until smooth:

¼ C pecans (soaked)
¾ C cashews
4 Medjool dates
1 ½ inch vanilla bean (or 1 ½ t pure vanilla extract)
1 ½ C water (or 1 C water and 8 ice cubes)
Meat from one coconut (optional – makes it more creamy)

Then add the following and blend again:

1 or 2 frozen bananas
¾ to 1 quart blueberries, frozen

Serve in a decorative glass and enjoy!

Raspberry Coconut Smoothie

Blend in Vita-Mix or blender until smooth and creamy:

    1 frozen banana
    meat from one coconut
    1 C almonds, soaked
    2 C raspberries
    2 C peaches
    4 Medjool dates
    1 ½ C water

Serve with banana, apricots, blueberries or other favorite fruit. Extra tasty with a nut cream on top. (See Nut Creams section starting on p. 168.)

Blueberry Pear Smoothie

This smoothie has a terrific pudding-like consistency.

    1 small banana
    ½ quart frozen pears
    2" vanilla bean
    meat from 1 coconut
    1 C blueberries
    ¾ C water

Blend thoroughly in Vita-Mix or blender.

Strawberry Smoothie

Put the following in the Vita-Mix or blender:

1 orange

2 cups frozen
    strawberries

1 banana

¼ cup almonds,
    soaked

4 Medjool dates

Blend until smooth. The orange usually adds enough liquid for this smoothie, but if using a regular blender, you may need to add water. Serve topped with a strawberry or add a dollop of cream. (See Nut Creams section starting on p. 168.)

Strawberry Peach Delight

1 C almonds, soaked
5 Medjool dates
1 ½ inches vanilla bean
1 C orange juice, preferably fresh squeezed
2 frozen bananas
2 C strawberries, frozen
2 C peaches, frozen

Blend in Vita-Mix until it looks like soft ice-cream.

Salads and Dressings

Tossed Salad

An extra-simple recipe to allow time for preparing other dishes.

    leaf lettuce
    tomatoes
    cucumbers (optional)

Sprinkle with fresh lime juice, olive oil, and salt.

Garden Salad

Start with these ingredients:

> leaf lettuce
> purple cabbage (small amount, shredded)
> carrots (grated finely)

Then add *several* of these choices to make a *really full*, flavorful salad:

> cucumbers, sliced
> celery (sliced fine)
> zucchini, grated (good in salads)
> cauliflower
> broccoli
> olives
> tomatoes
> red onion, small amount finely sliced
> spinach leaves
> green salad onions
> beets, grated (a small amount adds good flavor)
> sunflower seeds, sesame seeds
> flax seeds (finely ground)
> peas (frozen peas tossed on salad will thaw quickly)
> pumpkin seeds
> kidney beans, garbanzo beans*, black beans, any other beans
> snow peas
> alfalfa sprouts
> other sprouts (clover, radish, sesame seed, etc)
> raw asparagus, chopped
> corn (try freshly cut off the cob for great flavor)
> avocado

*Make your own garbanzo beans to avoid sulfites. Many canned garbanzo beans (also known as Chick Peas) are canned with sulfites to keep them light in color. MSG sensitive people are often sensitive to sulfites.

Ranch Dressing

Blend the following until smooth:

    1 C cashews*
    1-2 t salt
    1 t garlic powder
    1 t onion powder
    ¼ t thyme
    ¼ t rosemary
    ¼ t basil
    1 T lemon or lime juice
    1 C water**

At the end, add dill and stir in.

    1 T dill

Makes 1 ¼ C of dressing.

Salad

    romaine lettuce
    red bell pepper
    grated carrot
    grated zucchini, opt.
    olives

Variation: Add 1-3 t flax oil to above recipe before blending (adds good omega 3 fatty acids).

Note: Blending in the dill on high will make the dressing turn green. It looks more like Ranch Dressing if you wait until the end and just mix the dill in slowly. You can also blend on the slowest speed for a few seconds to just barely mix in the dill.

*Soaked for one hour. If you don't have time to soak them, just use a little more water.

** Add more water as needed for dressing consistency.

Greek Salad

Prepare ahead: You'll need ½ C cooked garbanzo beans for this recipe.

Add the following ingredients to a large salad bowl and mix together:

½ C garbanzo beans, drained (save juice for dressing)
½ large red onion (8 oz), chopped
½ large green pepper, chopped
3 Roma tomatoes, chopped
½ long English cucumber, chopped
½ head romaine lettuce, shredded (optional)
2 cloves garlic, minced
12 olives, chopped

1 recipe Greek Salad Dressing (below)

Greek Salad Dressing

Blend in blender until smooth:

¼ C juice from garbanzo beans (or use water)
1 T olive oil
⅓ C lemon juice
2 T honey
¼ t salt

Mix in dried oregano:

½ t oregano

Chill in refrigerator. Pour over Greek Salad and mix.

Raspberry Dressing

Blend the following until smooth:

¼ C oil
¼ C Medjool dates (or to taste to sweeten the dressing)
⅔ C fresh or frozen raspberries (packed)
1 T lemon juice
dash salt
½ C water

Serve over a fresh green leafy salad.

"Sour Cream"

Blend until smooth:

> ½ C cashews (soaked 1 hour)
> ½ C sunflower seeds, raw (soaked overnight)
> 1 ½ C water
> 2 T lemon juice
> 1 t onion powder
> ½ t garlic powder
> 1 t salt

Use in place of sour cream in many recipes, to top soups, on potatoes, etc.

Cheesy Sauce

Great as a dip, or cheesy topping for potatoes.

Blend the following until smooth:

    1 C almonds (or ¾ C almonds and ¼ C walnuts)
    1 C baby carrots
    1 ½ t salt
    2 t fresh garlic
    ¼ medium onion
    water (around 1 C*)

Then add:

    ½ t dill
    dash cumin, optional
    dash rosemary, optional

This and the next recipe are both good for dipping raw vegetables like cucumbers, zucchini, and carrots. Both sauces also make great lettuce roll-ups (spread dip on lettuce, then add chopped carrot, onion, asparagus, pea pods, tomatillos, tomatoes... and roll up)!

*Amount of water needed varies depending on how dry the nuts are. Start with a little less than a cup and add water slowly until it blends smoothly.

Cheesy Sauce with Tomatoes

This tomato version is similar to the previous Cheesy Sauce, however it uses tomatoes for the liquid to add the orange-red color instead of carrots.

Blend the following:

    3 Roma tomatoes
    1 C almonds (or ¾ C almonds and ¼ C walnuts)
    1 T pine nuts, opt.
    2 t salt
    2 t fresh garlic
    ¼ medium onion

Then put in:

    ½ t dill
    dash cumin, optional
    dash rosemary, optional

Use for dipping veggies, on potatoes, in lettuce wraps, etc.

Guacamole

Blend until smooth:

> 2 medium avocados
> ¼ small-medium tomato
> nickel-sized slice of garlic clove
> ⅛ medium onion (3 T)
> 1 or 2 sprigs fresh cilantro
> 1 T lime juice
> 1 t salt
> ⅛ jalapeño pepper, deseeded

That's it! Very fresh tasting!

Variation: You can keep out tomato until after blending. Then chop tomato (use a whole tomato if you want) and add tomato chunks to the guacamole.

Tasty Italian Salad Dressing

Blend all ingredients until smooth.

$^1/_3$ C lemon juice (about 1 and a half lemons, or a little more)
½ C water
½ C sunflower oil (cold pressed)*
1 t flaxseed oil (opt.)
2 T honey (opt.)
3 T pine nuts
½ t ground flaxseed
2 ½ t salt
½ t fresh garlic (or 2 t garlic powder)
2 t onion powder
2 t dried parsley flakes
1 t oregano, dried (or 2 T fresh oregano)
1 t basil, dried (or 2 T fresh basil)
½ t marjoram

Optional:

dash thyme
dash dill
dash celery seed
dash ground mustard seed
dash paprika
dash cayenne pepper

*Any *mild* oil you like is fine. Cold-pressed oils are better for your health. Extra virgin olive oil has too strong of a flavor for most people in this recipe.

Quick Italian Salad Dressing

$^1/_3$ C lemon juice (about 1½ lemons, or a little more)
½ C water
½ C sunflower oil (cold pressed)*
2 T honey (opt.)
2 t salt
2 t garlic powder
2 t onion powder
2 t dried parsley flakes
2 ½ t Italian seasoning**

Put in a salad dressing bottle and shake well.

*Any *mild* oil you like is fine. Cold-pressed oils are better for your health. Extra virgin olive oil has too strong of a flavor for most people in this recipe.

**If you don't have Italian seasoning, use 1 t oregano, 1 t basil, and ½ t marjoram.

Peanut Sauce Dressing

Blend in Vita-Mix or blender till smooth.

1 C water
5 oz. young coconut meat (one young coconut)
½ C peanut butter (or almond butter*)
½ inch ginger root
1 inch square tamarind paste
⅓ C honey
2 T fresh lime juice
1 ¼ t salt
⅛ green jalapeño pepper**
OR ¼ t dried red peppers

This makes a great Thai style dressing! Use on the following salad, or use on a salad of your choice.

*Peanut sauce is more authentic using peanut butter. But for allergies, digestibility, variety or other reasons you may want to try almond butter.

**Use more or less jalapeño pepper, depending on how hot you like it! Take out the seeds for milder flavor.

Thai Salad with Peanut Sauce

Use the above Peanut Sauce Dressing over the following lettuce and cucumber salad:

lettuce, chopped
cucumbers, sliced

Optional:

tofu (sautéed)
tomatoes

Barbara's Favorite Romaine Salad

Wash lettuce leaves, cut along the rib line, then thinly slice it the other way (¼" to ½" wide strips).

    1 head Romaine lettuce

Add remaining ingredients to Romaine lettuce in a large salad bowl:

    2 - 3 carrots, finely grated (organic carrots taste sweeter)
    1 C thinly sliced red cabbage
    1 red bell pepper, diced
    1 C thinly sliced sweet onion (or other mild onions*)
    1 cucumber, thinly sliced
    1 C garbanzos or black beans, precooked
    OR ½ C walnuts, slivered almonds, or sunflower seeds, raw
    any other veggies you happen to have (tomatoes, avocado, etc.)
    Optional: alfalfa sprouts
           spinach

Toss salad and serve with your favorite salad dressing. Or use the Desperate Dressing below.

*Green onions also taste great, but white onions add a nicer color contrast.

Desperate Dressing

When desperate, in a hurry and you don't have time to make a dressing, here's a quick fix for a flavorful salad:

Sprinkle the following on your salad, toss a little and eat!

    flax oil
    salt
    onion powder

Thai Salad

Mix all ingredients together in salad bowl:

2 large cucumbers, chopped (long, thin strands)
scant ½ t salt
2 t honey
¼ – ½ jalapeño, deseeded, finely chopped (more or less depending on
    preference)
1 T lime juice
3 baby carrots, finely grated
½ - 1 Roma tomato, finely chopped
1 green onion, chopped

Let sit a few minutes if possible, then serve.

Honey Mustard Salad Dressing

Blend in Vita-Mix or blender until smooth:

⅔ C cashews
¼ C water
¼ C honey
¼ C lemon juice
¾ C olive oil
½ t salt
1 ½ T mustard seeds
1 T chopped fresh parsley
1 T chopped raw onion

Serve over baby greens, a romaine lettuce salad, or any other salad you like.

Thai Cucumber Salad/Salsa

1 small tomato
1 large cucumber, peeled
¼ medium onion (sweet onion is nice)
2 sprigs cilantro
1 T lime juice
½ t honey
½ t salt
¼ C sunflower seeds

Blend at very low speed in food processor or Vita-Mix until chopped in small chunks.

Fresh Salsa

Fresh salsa is much more flavorful than salsa from a jar!

Process the following in a food processor until only small pieces remain:

　　3 tomatoes, cut in fourths
　　1 clove garlic (or more if you love garlic)
　　¼ of an onion (a little more if using sweet onions)
　　1 t fresh jalapeño (cut a piece off the end)*
　　1 lime, juiced
　　1 t salt
　　¼ C fresh cilantro
　　1 C cabbage (optional)

Serve in tacos, with chips, on salads, or on baked potatoes.

Note: Make a lot of this during cold and flu season because fresh garlic has anti-viral, anti-bacterial *and* anti-fungal properties to boost the immune system. Fresh onion also is a strong cold and flu fighter. The tomatoes and lime have vitamin C. In addition, the fresh jalapeño keeps the circulation moving.

*Remove seeds to reduce heat. Add more jalapeño if you like it hot.

Avocado Lime Salad

4 Roma tomatoes (2 C)
6 T red onion, finely chopped
4 small avocados, chopped
1 lime, juiced
1 t salt

Mix together and serve.

Tomato Salad

4 large ripe tomatoes
½ C Sunflower Sour Cream (next page)
½ C chopped green onion (1 to 2 onions)
½ t salt or to taste

Stir all ingredients together in a bowl. Serve immediately.

Sunflower Sour Cream

Blend the following until smooth:

    1 C raw sunflower seeds
    1 C water
    4 T lemon juice, fresh squeezed (1 lemon)
    1 t salt
    ¼ t onion powder

Use in many recipes calling for sour cream or try it on a salad.

Variation: Try using cashews to replace half or all of the nuts.

Fresh Corn

A simple, tasty side dish. I didn't realize how delicious raw corn could be until I started eating this!

Cut raw corn off of cob. Place in bowl, add salt and stir.

    3 ears fresh corn on the cob (uncooked)
    ½ t salt or to taste

Serve as a sweet, crunchy side dish!

Variation: Add tomatoes, and a dollop of "Sour Cream" or Ranch Dressing. (See p. 50 & p. 47) If desired, also add raw asparagus, chopped.

Cucumber Dill Salad

Makes a fresh summer salad!

    2 large cucumbers, sliced
    juice of one lemon
    2 t dill
    1 t salt or to taste

Mix all ingredients together in a bowl.

Variation: Add any of the following ingredients to the above salad:

    a chopped green onion
    ¼ of a small red onion, sliced thinly
    ½ of a tomato, thinly sliced
    ½ C celery, thinly chopped

Sunflower Dip

Blend the following until smooth:

    1 C raw sunflower seeds
    1 T sesame seeds (optional)
    1 C water
    4 T lemon juice
    1 ½ t salt
    ¾ t onion powder
    ⅛ t garlic powder

Add dill and blend on slow speed:

    1 t dill

Use as a dip for veggies or chips.

Note: This is very similar to the Sunflower Sour Cream recipe (p. 64), except that sesame seeds, garlic powder and dill are added.

Simple Avocado Salad Dressing

Blend or mash the following:

    1 avocado
    ½ lime, juiced
    ¼ C water
    ⅛ t dill
    ¼ t salt

Toss with spinach and tomato salad, or serve with any salad.

Potato Salad

Boil 6-8 potatoes for use below. Boil just until tender but not mushy.

Blend:

> 2 C cashews
> 1 T lemon juice
> ½ t onion powder
> 1 t garlic powder
> 2 ½ t salt
> ⅛ t mustard (freshly ground mustard seed is nice)
> dash turmeric
> ¾ C water

Stir or blend in slowly:

> 1 T dill

Put the following in a bowl and add the above dressing:

> 6-8 potatoes, boiled and cooled (by running water over or refrigerating)
> 1-2 t salt
> 1 ½ C chopped dill pickles (or homemade pickles, made with lemon juice)
> ¼ C pickle juice (liquid out of pickle jar)
> ¼ red onion, finely chopped or other mild onion

Stir well and refrigerate until serving. If you like it cold, put in refrigerator or freezer for an hour or two.

Honey Mustard Potato Salad

Steam potatoes for 20 minutes or until tender. Briefly boil green beans for 2 minutes, then rinse in cold water.

Mix the following together in a bowl:

    1 pound red potatoes, boiled and chopped
    1 C fresh green beans, boiled for two minutes
    1 ½ C canned white beans, drained
    1 small red pepper, chopped
    ½ t salt

Then add the sauce (below) and mix together.

Honey Mustard Sauce:

Blend in Vita-Mix or blender until smooth:

    ⅔ C cashews
    ¼ C water
    ¼ C honey
    ¼ C lemon juice
    ¾ C olive oil
    ½ t salt
    1 ½ T mustard seeds
    1 T chopped fresh parsley
    1 T chopped raw onion

Serve immediately or chilled.

Cranberry Broccoli Salad

This salad is great for the Holiday Season!

Place the following in a large bowl. Use a food processor for easier shredding and chopping.

1 ¼ C fresh cranberries (chopped)
4 C shredded cabbage
1 C chopped walnuts
1 small onion finely minced
1 or 2 C chopped broccoli
½ C raisins

Blend the following and pour over salad:

⅞ C oil
dash salt
dash garlic powder
dash onion powder
1 T pecans
½ C honey or evaporated cane juice
2 T lemon juice

Serves 10 to 12. Great size for a family gathering!

Variation: Replace the above dressing with the following:

1 C cashews
dash salt
dash garlic powder
dash onion powder
5 Medjool dates (or ½ C honey)
2 T lemon juice
½ C water (or up to the top of the cashews in the blender or Vita-Mix)

Blend in Vita-Mix or blender. They are both very similar, but the oil is replaced with cashews.

Breads

Biscuits

This version uses nuts instead of oil for those who prefer a creamier biscuit and a more natural fat.

Mix the following in a Vita-Mix or blender:

½ C water
½ C chopped pecans or other nuts

Measure the flour into a bowl and stir:

2 C quinoa* flour
1 T tapioca flour
2 t baking powder
1 t salt

Mix all ingredients together in the bowl, adding extra water or flour as needed to make a thick dough. Form into small flat circles of dough and place on cookie sheet.

Bake at 400 for 20 minutes.

*Pronounced KEEN-wah.

Note on quinoa flour: Many health food stores carry alternative flours like this. Bob's Red Mill is a good source, also check Safeway or on the web. If the biscuits are **bitter** it means the quinoa flour was old. These flours go bad quickly and should be kept refrigerated or in a freezer until use. (Many grocery stores do not keep the flour cold so if it sits too long on the shelf it may be rancid or bitter. Look for an expiration date and let them know if you get a bad batch.)

Quick Biscuits

This version does not need a blender, so it is quicker.

Preheat oven to 425. Mix dry ingredients together in a bowl.

> 1 ½ C quinoa flour
> 1 T baking powder
> ½ t salt

Add oil and water, then stir, adding more liquid as needed.

> ⅜ C olive oil
> ¾ – 1 C water

Shape into 1 inch wide biscuits, about ½ inch high. Bake on cookie sheet for about 10 minutes.

Note: The small biscuits will bake quicker and lighter.

Banana Bread Muffins

Preheat oven to 400.

Blend in Vita-Mix or blender until smooth:

    1 ripe banana
    ⅝ C honey
    ½ C water
    ¾ C cashews
    1 t vanilla extract (or 1 inch vanilla bean)

Mix the following together in a large bowl:

    1 ¼ C quinoa flour
    2 T garbanzo flour
    1 t baking powder
    ½ t baking soda
    ½ t salt

Add the wet ingredients to dry ingredients and stir. Fold in nuts if desired:

    ½ C chopped walnuts (optional)

Spoon batter into oiled muffin pans, filling each about halfway.

Bake 15 minutes (or until edges begin to brown and centers are cooked through).
Makes 10 small muffins.

Teff Muffins

These are very good, light and tasty!

Preheat oven to 400. Combine the following dry ingredients in a bowl:

¾ C teff flour
¾ C rice flour
1 T tapioca flour
1 ½ t baking powder
½ t cinnamon
½ t salt

Blend the following:

2 T flax seed
1 C water
⅓ C olive oil
⅜ C honey

Stir everything together until smooth then add:

½ C chopped nuts (filberts, almonds, or pecans)

Oil muffin pans. Bake at 400 for 25 minutes. Makes about 8 muffins.

Blueberry Muffins

Blend the following in Vita-Mix or blender:

⅜ C oil
¼ C water
1 t liquid lecithin
¾ C honey (or 1 C fructose)
1 t vanilla extract
1 T Minute Tapioca
½ C cashews
1 ripe banana

Stir together in bowl:

1 ¾ C quinoa flour
1 t baking powder
½ t baking soda
½ t salt

Add the liquid mixture to the dry mixture in bowl and mix. Then stir in:

½ C blueberries, frozen or fresh

Pour into pan or muffin tins and bake at 375 for 17 minutes.

Banana Muffins

Preheat oven to 425. Mix the following dry ingredients:

½ C light buckwheat flour
1 – 1 ¼ C brown rice flour
2 t baking powder
1 ½ t cinnamon
½ t salt
½ t nutmeg
⅛ t ginger

Blend:

1 T flaxseed
1 C water

Then add the following to the blender and blend again briefly:

1 C banana, mashed
2 T vegetable oil
¾ C applesauce

Mix the wet and dry ingredients together and add:

½ – 1 C chopped nuts (pecans or walnuts or your favorite)

Bake 12 – 15 minutes at 425.

Cornbread

Mix together in bowl:

2 C cornmeal
1 C rice flour
2 T tapioca flour
4 t baking powder
2 t salt

Blend the following until smooth:

¾ C cashews
1 ½ C water
⅓ C honey

Add liquid to dry ingredients and pour into baking dish. Bake at 400 degrees for 15 to 20 minutes.

Rice Crackers

Stir the following ingredients together in a bowl:

1 ½ C rice flour
¼ C tapioca flour
¼ C sesame seeds
½ t salt

Add the oil and stir in with a fork.

3 T vegetable oil

Add enough water to form a soft dough.

⅔ C water

On a well-floured surface, roll out dough very thinly. Brush on a little extra oil and sprinkle salt on top. Cut into rectangles and place on baking sheet.

Bake at 425 for 8 to 15 minutes (depending on thickness of crackers). When golden brown, remove crackers from baking sheet to prevent over browning.

Variation: Replace rice flour with *light* buckwheat flour for crispy buckwheat crackers.

Corn Chips

Put the following in a bowl:

  2 C Masa flour* + ½ C if needed below
  1 C fine cornmeal

Blend in Vita-Mix or blender:

  ½ onion
  3 cloves garlic
  1 ½ t salt
  1 ½ C water

Add to flour mixture and stir. Add extra flour if needed to make stiff dough. If dough is sticky it needs more flour. If it's too crumbly add a little more water.

Roll thin and cut into triangles. Sprinkle with salt on top if desired.

Bake at 425 until crisp (check after 10 minutes; time will depend on thickness).

*Masa flour is very finely ground corn meal and is normally sold in the Mexican food section of grocery stores.

Entrées

Crusty Chili Casserole

Lightly oil a 9"x12" baking dish. Layer the following ingredients in the baking dish in the following order:

    1 onion, chopped
    2 jalapeños, deseeded (use only half for this layer, save rest for after corn)
    2 C black beans, or pinto beans
    ½ t salt or to taste
    1 C corn, frozen or fresh
    remaining chopped jalapeño from above

To make the crusty cornbread top, blend the following in Vita-Mix or blender:

    ⅓ C nuts
    1 ½ C water
    1 ½ t salt

Mix the following together in a bowl. Then stir in the wet mixture (above):

    2 ¾ C fine corn meal
    2 t cumin
    1 t oregano
    1 t garlic
    dash cayenne if desired

Spread cornmeal mixture over the other ingredients in the baking dish. Bake uncovered at 350 for one hour.

Potato Wedges

Mix all together in large bowl, coating potatoes evenly with oil and seasoning mixture.

  3 or 4 potatoes, chopped into wedges
  ⅛ C olive oil
  1 T salt
  1 ½ t parsley flakes
  ½ t garlic powder
  dash cayenne pepper

Spread out on oiled cookie sheet. Bake for 15 – 20 minutes at 425 until the edges begin to brown.

Serve with Sunflower Dip (p. 67) or ketchup.

Gravy

Cashew gravy is more similar to dairy gravies, and is great for sharing with any crowd. The Brazil nuts are also good, but have a little different flavor. We recommend using the cashews at first, then trying out other nuts as you feel adventurous.

Blend until smooth:

  4 C water
  ¾ C nuts (cashews, Brazil nuts...)
  2 t salt
  2 t garlic powder
  1 t onion powder
  ⅛ C rice flour (or dry brown rice if using Vita-Mix)

Cook in fry pan on medium-high until thick, stirring constantly.

Gravy on baked potatoes with some vegetables makes a delicious meal!

Variation: Makes a wonderful filling for pot pie.

Lazy man's note: if you can't stir constantly, just turn it down and stir occasionally.

Onion Gravy

Sauté onions until soft:

    1 large onion

Blend in Vita-Mix or blender until smooth:

    3 C water
    2 T rice flour (or 2 T dry rice if using a Vita-Mix)
    ¾ C cashews, soaked
    1 ½ t salt
    ⅛ t garlic powder

Add blended mixture to onion and simmer 5 minutes or until thickened.

Mashed Potatoes

This recipe uses a little olive oil to give the rich flavor instead of butter or margarine.

8 medium potatoes

Boil potatoes until soft when poked with fork. Pour off water and add the following:

¼ C extra-light olive oil*
1 T salt or to taste

Beat with mixer until fluffy. Extra tasty when served with cashew or Brazil nut gravy.

* Other mild-tasting oils may be substituted.

Mashed Potatoes and Gravy

This recipe combines the mashed potato and gravy recipes, but replaces the oil in the potatoes with a thick nut milk.

Boil potatoes until soft when poked with fork.

> 8 medium potatoes

Meanwhile, blend the following:

> 1 C nuts (cashews, Brazil nuts...)
> 1 ½ C water

Pour out ½ C of the thick milk and set aside for mashed potatoes.

For gravy, add the following to the nut milk in the Vita-Mix or blender:

> 3 C water
> 2 t salt
> 1T garlic powder
> 1T onion powder
> ¼ C rice flour (or hard brown rice if using Vita-Mix)

Blend until smooth and cook in fry pan on medium-high until gravy is thick, stirring constantly.

Back to the potatoes... Beat the following with mixer until fluffy:

> *Potatoes (from above)*
> *Thick nut milk (set aside previously)*
> 1 T salt or to taste

Serve potatoes topped with piping hot gravy and enjoy!

Split Pea Soup

3 C water
1 C split peas
1 t salt
1 t garlic powder
1 t onion powder

Boil approximately 1 hr and 15 min. until smooth and you can no longer see any individual peas.

Variation: Put the 3 C water in the Vita-Mix with a carrot or two and a piece of celery. Blend and cook this with the split peas and salt. Adds nice flavor to soup. Also you can add fresh onion and garlic to the Vita-Mix instead of using the powdered form.

Borscht

Russian beet soup.

Put the following ingredients in pot and simmer for 45 minutes:

    8 C water
    4 C shredded green cabbage
    1 C grated beet (coarsely grated)
    1 onion, chopped
    2 cloves garlic, finely chopped
    2 large potatoes, chopped
    2 T dried parsley
    2 T honey
    2 t dill
    1 t paprika

Then blend these items and pour them in the pot:

    ½ C nuts (cashews, Brazil nuts, almonds)
    1 C water (from the soup)
    2 t salt

Warm through. Serve with a dollop of "Sour Cream" if desired (see below).

"Sour Cream"

    1 C sunflower seeds or cashews (raw, soaked)
    1 ½ C water
    2 T lemon juice
    1 t onion powder
    ½ t garlic powder
    1 t salt

Blend until smooth.

Pizza

Finally, a wheat-free pizza crust with no MSG/sulfite thickeners! The variation at the end is even better!

Crust:
1 ½ C brown rice flour
½ C tapioca (ground into flour)
1 t salt
1 T baking powder
½ t honey
1 T oil
water

Heat oven to 425. Mix dry ingredients together. Add wet ingredients, using enough water to make a thick dough. Spread it out on an oiled cookie sheet and prebake for 15 minutes while preparing toppings. After the toppings are on, bake for 25 minutes.

Toppings:
spaghetti sauce or pizza sauce (buy a natural one, check ingredients for MSG)
olives
mushrooms
onions
bell pepper
Optional: spinach, cheesy sauce (p. 51), pineapple, tomatoes (after baking)

Savory Pizza Crust Variation: Add 1 t Italian seasoning (if you don't have it, add ⅛ t of the following: marjoram, thyme, rosemary, basil, savory, oregano, sage).

Note: This pizza tastes GOOD, but it is still NOT the same as regular pizza. We recommend trying recipes that are closer to what you are used to when you *first* switch to wheat, dairy, and/or MSG free foods. But after a few months, when those pizza cravings hit you, and others around you are enjoying pizza, then this recipe becomes extremely valuable.

We have tried to simplify this recipe as much as possible, but with the combinations of wheat and MSG allergies, there is currently no other option than to make your own crust. Also, there are no store bought cheese replacements that are completely dairy free *and* MSG free. But for saving time, just choose any quick item with **fat** (to replace the fat flavor in cheese); for example, add lots of olives (already chopped).

Veggie Pot Pie

A wonderful savory entrée for dinner.

Prepare your favorite **pie crust** ahead of time*. (Or make without a crust to save time.)

Pie Crust recipe*

GRAVY: Blend the following in Vita-Mix or blender until smooth (5 min):

½ C cashews
1 ¾ C water
1 T rice flour

Add the following seasonings to the blender:

1 med onion
2 cloves garlic
¼ t cumin
1 t paprika
2 t salt
1 t chicken seasoning (opt. see p. 166)

VEGGIES: In a large bowl mix the following veggies with the above gravy from the Vita-Mix or blender:

3 potatoes chopped
2 small carrots sliced
2 celery stalks chopped
1 bell pepper chopped
½ bag peas
½ bag corn

Pour into crust and bake at 400 for 45 to 50 minutes or until veggies are done.

Note: For faster cooking, steam veggies while making gravy, and bake at 425 for 30 to 40 minutes.

*See p. 179 for a pie crust recipe.

Garden Rice Casserole

Cook brown rice.

    6 C cooked brown rice

While rice cooks, blend the following to make a sauce:

    1 C sunflower seeds
    3 C water
    ½ large onion or 2 T onion powder
    2 t salt

Put the following in a large bowl:

    1 medium grated zucchini
    2 medium grated carrots
    ½ red bell pepper (chopped)
    1 large onion (chopped)
    1 clove garlic (minced)

Add brown rice and sauce to the veggies. Mix and pour into an oiled casserole dish. Bake at 350 for approximately 30 minutes.

Pecan Rice Casserole

Blend the following until smooth and milky looking:

  1 C pecans
  5 C water
  2 t salt
  1 T onion powder
  ¼ t garlic powder

Put *dry* rice in a 9" x 13" casserole dish. Add above liquid mixture and asparagus or other vegetable. Stir.

  2 C brown rice (*un*cooked)
  2 – 3 C asparagus or other vegetable (chopped)

Bake at 400 for 45 – 50 minutes (until rice is done).

Miang Kham (Thai Lettuce Bites)

SAUCE: Blend in Vita-Mix or blender until smooth to make the sauce:

½ can coconut milk*
3 T ginger
2 – 3 T tamarind paste**
2 T shallots (or red onion)
1 ½ t salt
1 C honey
½ C liquid (water or broth)

FILLINGS: The following ingredients will be the fillings:

roasted peanuts
roasted dried grated coconut
lime, with peel (finely chopped)
ginger (finely chopped)
jalapeño pepper (finely chopped)
red onion (finely chopped)

Wrapping:

large lettuce leaves (washed)

Place a little of each filling in a lettuce leaf and pour sauce over the top. Roll up and take a bite. Delicious bursts of flavor in every bite!

*Highly sensitive individuals may need to watch for sulfites, extracts and thickeners in coconut milk.

**Look for tamarind paste at Asian food stores.

Pineapple Stir Fry

Stir fry in deep fry pan or wok until just tender:

    2 C cooked brown rice
    ½ fresh pineapple, in chunks (or 1 can pineapple*)
    ½ to 1 C peas
    2 carrots, chopped
    1 onion, chopped
    2 cloves garlic, minced
    1 bell pepper, chopped
    shredded coconut (optional)
    green beans (optional)
    salt to taste

Be sure to remove from burner early. It will continue to cook for a few minutes after removing from stove. *Lightly* cooked veggies taste great!

*Watch for citric acid in canned pineapple if MSG sensitive.

Indian Style Potatoes with Spinach

Cook diced potatoes in 2 ½ quarts of boiling water for 6 minutes. Drain.

    5 medium Yukon Gold or red potatoes, diced (New potatoes are the best!)

Meanwhile, heat oil in a fry pan. Sauté mustard seeds for a few seconds until they pop. Add onion and garlic. Fry 3 – 4 minutes on medium.

    ¼ C oil (or a little more)
    ½ t whole mustard seeds

    1 large onion
    2 cloves garlic

When onions have light brown edges, add the following:

    Potatoes from above
    1 lb. fresh spinach (or frozen), chopped
    1 t curry powder (or garam masala)
    ⅛ t chili powder
    dash of cumin
    1 ½ T salt

Stir fry 5 to 10 minutes or until heated through and spinach *barely* starts to wilt. Serves 5.

Honeydew Boats

An easy fun dish for a *light* meal.

    1 honeydew melon
    1 C blueberries (fresh or frozen)
    ½ - 1 C raspberries (fresh or frozen)
    1 banana (sliced)

Cut melon in half, scoop out seeds. Toss berries and banana in melon halves and serve! Cream on top is delightful (see below)!

If time permits, scoop melon into small balls, mix with berries and banana and use melon rinds as bowls.

Cream:

    1 C almonds or cashews (or half of each)
    4 Medjool dates
    1 inch vanilla bean
    COLD water up to the top of the nuts (may add a little more while blending)
    ½ frozen banana (optional)

Place in Vita-Mix or blend and blend until smooth. Be sure to watch to see if it gets too thick and add more water so that it can process smoothly.

Why is this in the entrees section? Because FRUIT can make a good MAIN COURSE as well, not just a dessert or a side dish. It's a great way to make get more fruit into the diet.

Rice Bean Delight

You will need cooked rice for this recipe.*

Sauté the following in a fry pan:

    1 T oil
    ½ onion
    2 large cloves fresh garlic

Blend the following just until chunky in Vita-Mix or blender, then add to fry pan:

    $^1/_{16}$ jalapeño pepper (¼ t)
    3 tomatoes (Roma or other)

Add to fry pan:

    1 can pinto beans
    1-2 C rice, cooked
    ½ t cumin
    ¼ t Italian seasoning
    ¼ t rosemary
    1 t salt
    ½ t basil
    ½ t grated fresh ginger
    ⅛ t paprika

Cook a few minutes. Slice fresh tomatoes and place them in the bottom of a bowl to line it. Pour above mixture into bowl. Add a few sliced tomatoes to the top as decoration.

    3 or 4 more tomatoes

* White rice can cook in 20 minutes while you prepare the rest of the dish. Brown rice takes longer, so you may want to prepare it ahead. (Cooked rice can also be frozen and kept on hand.)

Falafels

Garbanzo patties for pita bread, or tasty plain.

Patties: Blend (in Vita-Mix or blender) until a few small chunks remain:

> 2 C chick peas, cooked & drained (save 1 T liquid)
> 1 T chick pea stock (or water)
> 1 onion, chopped enough to blend
> ¼ C parsley
> 3 garlic cloves

Then add:

> ½ t baking soda
> 1 t coriander
> 1 t cumin
> 1 ½ t salt or to taste
> 2-4 T rice flour (for thickening)

Form into 12 patties and place on an oiled cookie sheet. Bake at 375 for 20 to 30 minutes or until lightly browned*. (Prepare falafel toppings while baking. See below.)

Assembly: Put a falafel patty or two in a large lettuce leaf (or pita pocket). Top with chopped tomatoes, onion.

> 6-8 large lettuce leaves
> 2 large tomatoes, chopped
> ½ an onion, sweet or red, chopped

Serve with Falafel Topping (p. 101) or Falafel Tahini Sauce (p. 102).

Variation: Top with salad onions, lettuce, sprouts and/or cucumbers.

*Stove top method: Fry in hot, oiled frying pan. until golden-brown on both sides.

Falafel Topping

Blend the following in Vita-Mix or blender until smooth:

2 Roma tomatoes
⅛ fresh jalapeño pepper or ⅛ t dried chili powder (or to taste)
1 small onion
1 clove garlic
¼ t caraway seeds
1 t salt
½ t cumin
¼ t coriander

Serve over falafels.

Falafel Tahini Sauce

Blend the following until smooth:

  ⅛ jalapeño pepper
  4-5 cloves garlic
  1 ½ C sesame seeds
  1 t salt
  ½ t cumin
  ½ t coriander
  2 C water (approximately, should be sour cream consistency)

Pour over falafels.

Cream of Broccoli Soup

Simmer the following in a pot for 10 minutes:

    1 medium onion, diced
    3 C water

Meanwhile, blend the following until smooth:

    ¾ C cashews
    2 C water
    1 C cooked rice or 1 large potato or ¼ C rice flour

Add blended mixture and the following to the pot:

    6 C raw broccoli pieces
    1 ½ t salt
    1 t garlic powder
    1 t savory
    2 t chicken seasoning, optional (see p. 166)

Simmer until thick and broccoli is bright green*.

Serve hot! Serve with a salad or biscuits if desired**.

*Do not overcook; the broccoli will continue to soften after it leaves the stove.

**See Garden Salad p. 46 or biscuits p. 73.

Bursting Veggie Soup

A delicious, flavorful soup!

Boil potatoes until tender, then add other veggies.

> 1 potato, cubed
> water to cover potatoes
>
> ½ an onion, chopped
> 1 carrot, sliced
> ¼ crown broccoli, chopped (about 1 C)
> 1 – 2 C chopped cauliflower, chopped, optional
> 2 cloves fresh garlic, crushed

Add the following ingredients to Vita-Mix or blender and blend:

> *2 cups water taken out of boiling vegetables (above)*
> 1 C cashews
> 1 T salt
> 1 T garlic powder
> 2 t onion powder
> ¼ t thyme
> 1 T dill
> ⅛ t rosemary
> dash cayenne, optional

Blend until smooth and creamy and pour into the pot of potatoes and veggies. Cook until veggies are just tender, and creamy sauce is warm.

Creamy Fettuccine

Very good, flavorful fettuccine.

Noodles: Start water heating for noodles. Boil rice noodles according to package instructions.

  1 8-10 oz. package rice noodles

Sauce: Sauté onion in a large fry pan for 10 minutes, add celery and sauté 3 more min.

  2 medium Walla Walla sweet onions, chopped or one regular onion
  2 T oil

  3 stalks celery, chopped

Meanwhile, blend the following ingredients to make a sauce:

  ½ C Brazil nuts or cashews
  2 C water
  1 T onion powder
  ½ t garlic powder
  1 ½ t salt
  Optional: dill, basil, rosemary, thyme, up to ⅛ t each

Add blender mix to onions and celery, and heat. Pour sauce over noodles and serve.

Chili Salsa

This dish takes the flavors and aromas of chili and combines them with the fresh crunchy vegetables of summer. Use it as a salsa, dip or just eat it as a savory, cold, crisp summer soup or chili!

Blend the following:

⅛ Jalapeño pepper, deseeded
2 medium tomatoes
1 T cashews
1 Medjool date
2 t salt
1 C dried tomatoes*
5-8 baby carrots
½ C fresh cilantro
⅓ red onion
⅛ t cumin
¼ cucumber (the rest used below)
½ clove garlic
¼ t dried basil
½ large red pepper (the rest used below)

Then add the following, chopped in small chunks:

¾ cucumber
¼ large red pepper
1 green salad onion
1 tomato
optional: grated carrot
optional: 1 avocado
optional: half an ear of corn, uncooked

Serve at room temperature or cold in bowls with your favorite soup complementers (bread, corn chips, crackers, cucumber slices, avocados, popcorn...). Makes a flavorful, light summertime lunch. Or serve as dip with chips.

* If sensitive to mold or yeast, omit dried tomatoes.

Veggie Nut Balls

A lovely dehydrated nut ball. Tastes great with crunchy cucumber slices, sweet tomatoes and avocado slices.

Put the following ingredients through Champion-type juicer using blank plate to homogenize:

  1 C cashews
  2 C walnuts
  ½ C baby carrots
  3 stalks celery
  1 red pepper
  2 cabbage leaves
  1 small zucchini or ½ large zucchini
  1 Roma tomato

Add the following and mix everything together in a bowl:

  1 chopped green onion
  2 t salt
  1 T fresh rosemary, finely chopped
  1 clove garlic, finely chopped
  ¼ t dill
  1 t grated ginger
  ⅛ t cumin
  dash ground mustard seed

Make balls about an inch in size; dehydrate for four to eight hours*. Dip in your favorite sauce**.

*Dry one to two hours on a fruit leather tray (without holes), then transfer to a regular drying rack for the remainder of the time. You could also bake in oven at low temperature setting until dry.

**Try Sunflower Dip p. 67, Falafel Topping p. 101 Falafel Tahini Sauce p. 102 or Cheesy Sauce p. 51.

White Bean Dip

Add all the following ingredients to Vita-Mix or blender and blend:

    3 C white beans, cooked*
    ½ of an large onion
    4 cloves garlic
    1 T lemon juice
    1 T walnuts
    2 T sunflower seeds
    1-2 t salt or to taste

Serve immediately, or refrigerate.

Great with corn chips, rice crackers**, or veggies.

*1 ½ C dry beans, soaked overnight and then cooked. Or used canned beans.

**Feel free to buy your favorite corn chips or rice crackers. Plain ones usually do not contain MSG. Flavored chips and crackers often do, so read labels. See p. 81 and p. 80 to make your own.

Spicy Black Bean Dip

You will need 3 C black beans*, cooked well. Save liquid for blending.

Blend the following together in Vita-Mix or blender until smooth, adding liquid as needed:

    ¼ C almonds, soaked
    ¼ C dried pitted prunes (soaked if not soft)
    liquid from beans (maybe ½ C)

Add the following to the almond liquid and blend again:

    ½ small onion
    1 ½ T salt
    2 cloves garlic
    ½ jalapeño pepper, deseeded (optional)
    $1/16$ t cayenne, 40 heat (optional)

Add beans and blend until smooth:

    3 C black beans, cooked well

It's ready to use as a dip! Can be served warm, or cool as desired.

Great with corn chips, rice crackers**, or veggies.

*1 ½ C dry beans, soaked overnight and cooked, or use canned beans. Another option is to make beans ahead and freeze them.

**Feel free to buy your favorite corn chips or rice crackers. Plain ones usually do not contain MSG. Flavored chips and crackers often do, so read labels. See p. 81 and p. 80 to make your own.

Dahl

Boil in a large pot 45 – 60 minutes or until lentils are tender:

    1 C lentils
    2 C water

Sauté in fry pan briefly (30 seconds or until you smell the seasonings):

    2 T oil
    ½ t cumin seeds
    ½ t mustard seeds
    ½ t turmeric
    ½ t garam masala
    1 to 2 inches fresh ginger, chopped fine
    1 clove garlic, minced

Add the following and sauté until onions are tender (about 4 minutes):

    1 onion, chopped
    2 small tomatoes, chopped
    1 jalapeño, deseeded* and diced
    1 ½ t salt

Add lentils to fry pan. Simmer for 5 to 10 minutes to further soften lentils and blend flavors. Garnish with cilantro if desired.

* Deseeding still adds nice flavor, but much less heat. For a hotter Dahl, put in the seeds as well.

Baked Potato Bar

1 medium-sized potato per person*

Bake at 350 for an hour or more (until soft when poked with fork, less time for small potatoes)

Toppings for potatoes:

  2 large onions, chopped (stir-fry slowly until well done, approx. 30 min.)
  6 mushrooms, optional (stir-fried with onions)
  1 recipe nut gravy **
  2-4 C chili beans ***
  3-4 large tomatoes, chopped
  3 green salad onions, chopped
  ½ C each of parsley, cilantro and/or chives, chopped
  2 C olives, chopped
  1 head lettuce & 1 carrot grated****
  1 to 2 heads broccoli, chopped and steamed*****
  salad dressing (p. 47), cheesy sauce (p. 51) and/or salsa (p. 61)

Serve buffet-style with potatoes first. Pile on your favorite toppings and enjoy!

This works really well for a meal with friends! The Host/hostess can bake potatoes, and each contributor can easily prepare a couple toppings to bring along.

*Recipe serves 4 to 6.

**At least 3 C or more if you love gravy!

***You can use canned beans, or make large batch ahead and freeze in small containers.

****Can serve as a simple side salad or on potatoes.

*****Make last because broccoli cooks quickly and gets cold quickly also.

Gravy with Veggies

Blend the following and set aside:

> 2 ½ C water
> ½ C nuts (cashews, Brazil nuts...)
> 2 t salt
> 2-3 cloves garlic
> 3 T rice flour or raw brown rice if using Vita-Mix.

Sauté onion for 3 – 4 minutes, then add celery and carrots and sauté for an additional 2 – 4 minutes*.

> 1-3 T oil
> 1 onion, chopped
>
> 1-2 stalks celery, chopped
> ½ a large carrot, chopped

Add the blended mixture to the veggies. Simmer until it starts to thicken, stirring frequently.

Remove from heat and stir in:

> 2-3 C fresh spinach, chopped
> ½ C fresh cilantro, chopped (optional)

Serve immediately while veggies are hot and slightly crisp and spinach is just starting to wilt.

Serve over:

> steamed or boiled potatoes
> rice noodles (follow package directions)
> green bean threads or glass noodles

*Note: Veggies should be somewhat crisp at this point. They will still soften while the sauce thickens, and they are nice if served while just barely crunchy.

Green Chili Enchiladas

Whiz in Vita-Mix or blender and set aside for sauce:

  1 jalapeño deseeded
  ¼ onion
  1 clove garlic
  1 C cashews
  1 C Brazil nuts
  ⅛ C rice, dry (or ⅛ C rice flour)
  1 ½ to 2 t salt
  1 ½ C water

Sauté:

  1 med onion, chopped
  2 stalks celery, chopped

Warm in skillet:

  6 corn tortillas

Pour a little sauce in a 9 x 9 baking dish. Then put sautéed mixture with a little sauce in each tortilla. Roll them up and place in the baking dish. Pour remaining sauce over the top and bake for 20 minutes at 350.

Black Beans

Put the following in a pressure cooker*:

 3 C dry black beans, soak overnight or for several hours
 4 cloves fresh raw garlic chopped or minced
 1 onion, chopped
 ½ to 1 Jalapeño pepper, deseeded, minced
 ½ t cumin
 5 sprigs fresh cilantro, chopped
 1 Roma tomato, chopped
 water to ½ inch above level of beans

Pressure cook* for 6 minutes on high. Allow to pressure release naturally, roughly 20 minutes. (See your pressure cooker's guidelines for recommended cooking time, and add extra time to make sure they are well cooked.)

After cooking then add:

 1 T salt

Stir in and allow a sit or simmer for a few minutes to allow flavors to seep in.

Serves 8 to 10. Very nice on potatoes topped with salad and ranch dressing.

*If you don't have a pressure cooker, bring to a boil, then simmer on stove for an hour to an hour and a half. Or you can use a crock pot and simmer them all day.

Note: Beans are much tastier when well cooked. If cooking on the stove, be sure that they are WELL done and very soft. There is a strong tendency to under cook beans, and you can be known for great beans if you cook them a little extra.

When transitioning to a healthier diet, the second secret in making great beans is to add enough salt. (Over time you may find you don't need as much salt.) When possible, make them ahead so flavors will soak into the beans. Beans freeze well, for quick additions to meals.

Potato-Curry Stew

Recipe for pressure cooker:

  2 medium potatoes, cubed
  1 large carrot, cut up
  2 stalks celery, cut up
  1 onion, cut up
  1 T curry paste (½ to 1 T depending on taste)*
  2 pieces star anise
  ½ t garlic powder
  1 t salt
  2 C water

High pressure for 6 minutes.

Remove about a cup of the soup liquid plus some chunks and put in Vita-Mix. Add the following nuts and blend:

  ¼ C cashews
  ¼ C Brazil nuts

Add the creamy liquid mix back into soup.

Serve with rice on the side.

*See p. 121 for Red Curry Paste recipe.

Tofu Steaks with Spinach

Sauté the following for two minutes:

> 1 T olive oil
> 1 C sliced red onion
> 1 C celery, sliced
> 2 cloves garlic, pressed
> 1 t ginger root, grated
> ¼ jalapeño pepper, deseeded

Add the following and cook for 2 minutes:

> 9 C spinach, chopped
> 2 C bell pepper, deseeded, deribbed and sliced

Mix the following with a wire whisk, and add to the stir-fry mixture:

> 2 C water or vegetable broth
> 2 T rice flour
> 1 t salt

Fry sliced tofu until golden-brown:

> 15 oz tofu, cut in slices

Serve spinach mixture on top.

Winter Baked Pasta

Prepare pasta and squash ahead of time.

Toss the following in a bowl:

> 6 C hot cooked Rigatoni or other medium shaped pasta
> 3 C butternut squash cooked, peeled, and cubed (or any winter squash)
>
> 3 C raw broccoli florets, chopped (about 1 lb.)
> 3 green onions, chopped
> 2 medium stalk celery, chopped fine

Blend the following sauce in Vita-Mix or blender until smooth. Add to bowl and stir:

> 1 t ground nutmeg
> 2 cloves garlic, pressed
> 1 C cashews
> ¼ C walnuts
> 2 t salt
> 2 C water

Pour into a lightly greased 3-quart casserole dish. Bake for 35 minutes at 375.

Side dish idea: this would go well with a huge green salad (p. 46) or fresh tomatoes.

Tomato Veggie Stir Fry

Begin cooking noodles according to package directions (if using noodles).

   Rice fettuccine noodles, optional

Sauté onion and garlic on medium for about 5 minutes, or until tender.

   1 T olive oil
   1 small onion, thinly sliced
   1 clove garlic, pressed

Add the following and sauté for 5 minutes or until peppers are tender:

   1 large green bell pepper, deseeded, deribbed and sliced
   4 ounces tofu, chopped (optional)

Add the following and simmer for 5 minutes:

   2 C diced tomatoes (approx. 4 Roma tomatoes)
   1 T lemon juice
   1 t oregano
   1 t tomato paste
   ¼ C water if needed
   1 t honey
   2 t salt

Serve this alone or with rice fettuccine noodles.

Red Beans and Rice

Prepare ahead tip: Soak beans overnight.*

If brown rice is desired, prepare ahead.

Sauté the first group of ingredients until onion begins to turn clear. Add remaining ingredients and cook in a pot on the stove for around 1 ½ hours. The beans should be very soft. If unsure, cook a little longer, since they are better *well* cooked than partially hard.**

2 T vegetable oil
1 medium onion, chopped
2 medium stalks celery, chopped
1 large green bell pepper, deseeded, deribbed and chopped
2 cloves garlic, pressed

3 ½ C water
3 C vegetable broth (or additional water)
1 lb. dried red beans (soaked overnight).

2 ½ t salt (add when nearly done cooking)

Add salt and serve.

Meal suggestions: Serve over brown rice. Add a big salad (p. 57) and some muffins (p. 76).

*Soaking helps beans cook more evenly and helps digestion. If you didn't have time to soak they will still work fine, just make sure they are thoroughly cooked before serving.

**For faster cooking, use pressure cooker on high for 6 minutes or according to manufacturer's instructions (allow 20-30 minutes for total cooking and pressure release time). Or cook in crock pot for 8-10 hours (MSG sensitive people should choose the faster cooking options since slow cooking frees up some natural glutamic acid).

Root Vegetables in Red Curry

Chop root vegetables ahead. Cook your favorite rice.

Sauté the following ingredients for 3 minutes:

   3 T vegetable oil
   ½ large onion (1 ½ C or 8 oz.)
   2 large cloves garlic, minced
   1 T Red Curry Paste*

Stir in the following until potatoes have browned slightly, about 4 minutes:

   1 ¾ C yam, peeled and cubed
   2 C golden sweet potato, peeled and cubed
   2 ¾ C baking potatoes, peeled and cubed
   1 lemon grass stalk, chopped in 1 inch pieces

Add water and cook until veggies are tender:

   1 C water

Stir in cashew milk and salt. Cook one more minute:

   1 C thick cashew milk (½ C cashews and ¾ C water, blended well)
   2 t salt

Serve over rice.

Lemon grass is for flavoring only; it should be removed before serving. Asian food stores carry it.
*See Red Curry Paste recipe (next page) or use your favorite.

Red Curry Paste

Blend the following together in a blender until smooth:

½ C onions, chopped
8 cloves garlic
10 dried jalapeño chilies (red)
4 inches fresh (or frozen) ginger root
2 T lemon grass, chopped
1 T cilantro, chopped
1 t salt

Optional:
2 T coriander seed
½ t paprika
½ t fennel seed
1 small sprig Thai Basil

Refrigerate for up to 1 month. May be frozen longer*.

*When frozen I can still manage to scrape off a small amount for a recipe by using a spoon or a small knife.

Pineapple Curry

Quick and easy, and tastes so good!

Start preparing your favorite rice*.

Sauté the following for just a minute or until you smell the curry paste.

> 1 T Red Curry Paste (see p. 121)
> 2-3 T coconut milk (the rest of the can used below)**

Add the following.

> *The remainder of the can of coconut milk*
> 1 can pineapple chunks with juice (or 1 ½ C fresh pineapple, chopped)***
> 1 t salt or to taste

Simmer for 10 to 15 minutes until warmed through and thickened just slightly.

Serve over rice!

*Thai Jasmine rice and Basmati rice are very good. Choose white or brown. (See p. 123 for more info.)

**Some canned coconut milk contains sulfites (metabisulfite, or anything ending in sulfite) or other additives(any extract, or any kind of gum) that bother MSG sensitive individuals. Check ingredients carefully. Some people make coconut milk from blending mature coconut meat, and straining. Search the Internet for more details if you can't tolerate canned coconut milk.

***Canned pineapple juice may have citric acid which usually contains traces of MSG, so highly sensitive individuals may prefer fresh pineapple.

Squash Curry

A very tasty Thai Curry!

Start preparing your favorite rice*.

Steam squash until tender. Allow to cool, and cut into chunks.

   1 squash, cut in half, seeds removed (use acorn, butternut, or Hubbard squash)

Sauté the following for a minute or until you smell the curry paste.

   1 T Red Curry Paste**
   2-3 T coconut milk (the rest of the can used below)**

Add the following and simmer for 10 to 15 minutes until slightly thickened.

   The rest of the coconut milk
   The squash from above
   1 cinnamon stick
   1 t salt or to taste

Remove cinnamon stick before serving. Serve over rice!

*Choose any rice you like. My favorite rice is Thai jasmine rice. It's used in many Thai restaurants because it has great texture and flavor. If you are not too fond of common brown rice, you might consider Basmati rice because of its higher quality and nicer flavor. Thai Jasmine brown rice has a very nice flavor, texture and aroma, if the brown reddish color does not deter you.

**See p. 121 for curry paste recipe.

***Some canned coconut milk contains sulfites (metabisulfite, or anything ending in sulfite) or other additives (any extract, or any kind of gum) that bother MSG sensitive individuals. Check ingredients carefully. Some people make coconut milk from blending mature coconut meat, and straining. Search the Internet for more details if you can't tolerate canned coconut milk.

Curried Winter Squash Soup

Bake the squash at 350 degrees until tender (around 45 minutes).

> 1 medium butternut squash*

Sauté the following until onion softens.

> 2 T oil
> 1 medium onion, chopped (12 oz.)
> 1 t curry paste**

Add the following and simmer for 15 minutes:

> *Squash from above*
> 2 medium apples, cored, peeled and chopped
> ½ t dried thyme
> 1 quart vegetable broth or water
> 2 t salt

Blend any remaining chunks with a little liquid until smooth.

Add cream (below) to soup, stir and serve!

Cream: Blend until smooth:

> 1 C cashews
> ¾ C water

*Cut squash in half and scoop out seeds. Turn cut side down on baking sheet (to keep moisture in). Sprinkle a little water over it or let it sit in a ½ inch of water for added moisture.

**See p. 121 for curry paste recipe.

Spicy Bean Tacos

Sauté the following until soft:

    1 T oil
    1 medium onion, chopped
    ½ jalapeño, deseeded and minced

Add the following and simmer for 10 minutes:

    ½ t garlic powder
    1 t ground cumin
    1 19 oz. can pinto beans or 2 ¼ C homemade pinto beans

Warm the corn tortillas and chop the toppings.

    12 corn tortillas
    ½ to 1 head lettuce, shredded
    4 tomatoes (or 8 Roma tomatoes), chopped
    3 ripe avocados, chopped
    Salsa (p. 61 or your favorite)

Spoon the bean mixture over the tortillas. Top with: lettuce, tomatoes, avocados, and salsa.

Homemade Pinto Beans

Cook in electric pressure cooker on high pressure for 9 minutes. Allow to cool down naturally. (It is better to cook a little extra than to have firm beans.)

    2 C dry pinto beans*
    6 C water (5 C if you soaked beans overnight)
    ½ large onion, chopped, optional
    1 clove garlic, chopped, optional
    ¼ jalapeño, deseeded and finely chopped (optional for a slight chili flavor)

When beans are tender, add salt.

    2 t salt

Serve immediately! **

*Soaked over night is preferable. Cover with fresh water at least an inch higher than bean level. Rinse and drain in the morning (or roughly 8 or so hours later). Soaking helps the beans cook more evenly and helps digestion. But if you didn't have time for soaking, the recipe will still be fine.

**If you have time, you can cook them a little extra to allow salt to seep into beans. Refrigerating overnight will also allow flavors to seep into beans.

NOTE: You can use this same recipe with other beans, like red beans, navy beans, baby Lima beans, white beans, garbanzo beans, etc.

Or cook in crock pot for 8-10 hours (MSG sensitive people should choose the faster cooking options since slow cooking frees up some natural glutamic acid). On the stove, cook roughly 1 ½ hours.

Double Baked Potatoes

Prepare ahead: Bake Potatoes at 350 for an hour. Buy or make black beans.

Cut potatoes in half lengthwise and scoop out the middle, leaving a ¼ inch shell. Place potato centers in a bowl and set aside. Bake shells in oven at 400 for 10 to 15 minutes until they start to brown on edges.

   6 large baked potatoes

Blend the following together until smooth:

   1 ½ C cashews
   ½ C walnuts
   1 ½ C water
   1 T lemon juice
   1 ½ t salt
   ½ t garlic powder
   ¼ t onion powder
   ½ t basil

Sauté the onion and broccoli. Mix the following, together in the bowl with the potato centers:

   1 C onion, chopped and sautéed briefly
   ½ C broccoli (or red pepper), chopped and sautéed briefly
   1 ½ C black beans
   Potato centers from above
   Cream from blender above

Fill the potato shells with the filling. Bake another 10 minutes until heated through.

   ¾ C salsa, optional

Top each potato with a little salsa* if desired.

*See page 61 or purchase a natural salsa.

Moo Shu Stir Fry

Sauté the following for one minute:

    1 t sesame oil
    1 t vegetable oil
    1 T ginger root, grated
    2 cloves garlic, pressed

Add cabbage and bell pepper and sauté another 2 minutes:

    5 C cabbage, thinly sliced
    1 C red bell pepper, deseeded and thinly sliced

Add the following:

    1 C green onions, sliced diagonally
    2 T lemon juice
    2 T water
    1 ½ t salt

Wrap ingredients in tortillas and top with salsa*.

    6 corn tortillas, warmed

*Optional. Use your favorite or see page 61 for fresh salsa.

Ratatouille

Prepare brown rice. Put the following ingredients in a pan or crock pot:

1 28-oz. jar/can spaghetti sauce*
1 large eggplant, chopped and peeled
2 large tomatoes, chopped large
2 large zucchini, sliced
1 large onion, chopped
3 cloves garlic, minced
1 t basil
1 t oregano

Cook in a covered pan for ½ hour or until vegetables are tender.

Serve over brown rice.

*Note: Many spaghetti sauces contain MSG, but organic ones are more often safe. Watch for natural flavors, spices, citric acid, modified food starch (modified anything), or anything hydrolyzed as these may indicate hidden MSG. See list of hidden sources of MSG on msgmyth.com.

Indian Okra Curry

This is a pretty fast curry recipe.

Sauté the following ingredients until they start popping:

    1 T oil
    1 t whole cumin
    1 t whole brown mustard seeds

Add the following and cook half a minute:

    1 t ground cumin
    1 t ground coriander
    1 t garam masala*

Add onion and sauté until half done:

    1 diced onion

Add the remaining ingredients and cook until everything is soft and starting to mush together a bit.

    1 - 16 oz bag of frozen cut okra (can be found at Super Wal-Mart)
    2 C diced tomatoes, fresh or from a can
    1 ½ t salt

Serve on rice.

*Indian spice mixture. You can buy it at Indian grocery stores or online, or make your own (search Internet for recipes). This amount won't make the curry very spicy. Add more if you like or some cayenne if you like spicy food.

Tofu Stuffed Eggplant

Trim off ends of eggplants and cut in half lengthwise. Discard seed sacks and scoop out flesh leaving ¼ inch shell*.

Three 1 ½ lb. eggplants

Sauté the following until tender (preheat oven to 350):

chopped eggplant flesh (from above)
1 T olive oil
½ lb. mashed firm tofu
1 C finely chopped mixed vegetables
⅓ C pine nuts
2-3 C brown rice, cooked
½ t salt

Sprinkle salt in eggplant shells. Fill eggplants with the sautéed mixture and bake for 30 minutes at 350 degrees.

* The skins may stay more firm by floating them in cold water.

Simply Smashing Stuffed Potatoes

Slice baked potatoes in half lengthwise and scoop out centers, leaving ¼ inch shell.

    4 medium Russet potatoes, baked

Beat the following with a mixer until light and fluffy:

    potato centers (from above)
    1 C soft tofu
    ¼ C green onion, diced
    1 ½ t chicken style seasoning*
    1 t salt
    1 t olive oil

Place mixture in potato shells and bake for 15 minutes at 350 degrees or until heated through.

*See recipe and comments page 166.

Chickpea and Vermicelli on Spinach

Cook chickpeas* ahead or use canned.

Cook vermicelli.**

   4 oz. green bean vermicelli

Combine the following in a bowl, then stir in the vermicelli:

   1 C chickpeas, warmed and drained
   ¼ C parsley, minced
   2 green onions, finely chopped
   ¼ C fresh lemon juice
   2 T olive oil
   2 cloves garlic, pressed
   1 t cumin
   1 t coriander
   1 t paprika
   ¼ t cayenne pepper or to taste
   2 t salt or to taste

Sauté spinach until wilted. Sprinkle with a little salt.

   1 bag fresh spinach

Serve spinach on plates topped with chickpea vermicelli mixture.

* Chickpeas are also known as garbanzos.
**Toss green bean vermicelli in boiling water and cook for 3 minutes or until soft.

Vegetable Pav Bhaji

This is very flavorful, a great way to eat vegetables!

You will need a seasoning called Pav Bhaji Masala. See note below.

Sauté until onions are brown, then stir in tomatoes and cook until thick:

    2 T olive oil
    2 cloves garlic, minced
    1 t green chili peppers, minced
    1 C onions, chopped
    2 t fresh ginger, grated

    1 C Roma tomatoes, chopped (about 2 tomatoes)

Stir in the following and cook for 15 minutes:

    2 C cauliflower, chopped
    1 C cabbage, chopped
    1 C green peas
    1 C carrots, grated
    4 potatoes, boiled and mashed
    1 ½ T pav bhaji masala*

Stir in salt and lemon juice and serve:

    1 T salt
    1 T lemon juice

*A spice popular in India. You may find it at an Indian Asian food store. Also check the Internet, or look for recipes to make your own (on the Internet also).

Cauliflower Pav Bhaji

A delicious Indian dish from Bombay area. You'll never know you're eating cauliflower!

Boil cauliflower and potatoes until tender and set aside.

> 1 head cauliflower, chopped into florets
> 4 – 5 medium potatoes

Sauté the following in a sauce pan:

> 3 T oil
> 1 green bell pepper, minced
> 1 clove garlic, minced
> 1 t fresh* ginger, minced

Add the following to the sauce pan:

> 3 C tomato puree (blend 8 Roma tomatoes or buy canned puree)
> ½ t turmeric
> ½ to 1 t red chili paste (to taste) or ½ t chili powder
> 2 t pav bhaji masala** (or to taste)
> 2 t salt

Keep simmering and mashing it together until mostly mashed, adding water as needed. For faster mashing, blend cauliflower and potatoes with a little water on low speed until partially mashed.

Feel free to adjust the amount of the masala until you like the balance between the tomato tang and the heat of the masala.

*We freeze ginger in 1" chunks to use when we are out of fresh ginger.

** Indian food stores sell pav bhaji masala, a dry mix of around 18 spices. May order on the Internet.

Wild Rice and Papaya Salad

Prepare ahead: cook wild rice and black beans.

Combine the following in a bowl:

    2 C black beans, drained and chilled
    3 C cooked wild rice, chilled
    1 C walnuts, chopped
    ¼ C red onion, chopped
    1 C fresh pineapple, cubed and chilled
    ½ t salt

Combine in a jar, shake well, then stir in with the above ingredients:

    ⅓ C lemon juice
    2 T olive oil
    2 t honey

Arrange spinach leaves on dinner plates and top with bean and rice mixture.

    ½ lb. spinach leaves

    1 papaya, sliced
    1 C strawberries, sliced

Decorate with sliced papaya and strawberries.

Italian Lentil Stew

Put the following in a slow cooker, pressure cooker or pot on the stove:

  1 ¾ C dried lentils
  1 small butternut squash, chopped in small chunks
  3 C spaghetti sauce (1 25 oz. jar or can)*
  2 C green beans, cut in half
  1 green bell pepper, diced
  1 large russet potato, diced
  1 onion, chopped
  2 cloves garlic, minced
  3 C water
  5 t salt

Cooking times are as follows. **Slow cooker:** on low for 8 to 10 hours or until the lentils are tender. **Pressure cooker:** 10 minutes on high pressure, letting it gradually cool down without releasing pressure, or 15 minutes when quickly releasing pressure. **Stove:** allow around an hour or more, or until vegetables are tender.

*Note: Many spaghetti sauces contain MSG, but organic ones are more often safe. See note p. 129.

Tasty Indian Cauliflower

Fantastic flavor; turns ordinary cauliflower into an exotic dish.

Sauté onion and garlic until soft. Then add the seasonings and sauté for 30 seconds more:

> 1 T oil
> 1 onion, peeled and chopped
> 2 – 4 garlic cloves
>
> 1 t ground cumin
> 1 t ground coriander
> 1 t yellow mustard seed
> ½ t turmeric

Add the cauliflower and water and simmer until tender. While simmering, toast the cashews for garnish (optional, see below).*

> 1 lb. cauliflower, cut into small florets
> 1 ½ C water
> ¼ C cashews, ground in the blender
> 1 t salt or to taste

Garnish with toasted cashews if desired. Serve with rice.

> ½ C toasted cashews (optional)*

*You can dry roast them in a small skillet on medium-low. Stir frequently so they don't burn.

Black Bean and Veggie Wraps

Warm tortillas:

    6 corn tortillas

Sauté the following about 4 minutes or until tender:

    1 medium onion, chopped
    2 C red bell pepper or 2 C mushrooms, chopped

Add the following and heat until spinach is wilted:

    2 C black beans (or 1 16 oz. can), drained
    4 C fresh spinach, chopped
    1 t salt or to taste
    ½ C olives, chopped

Serve on tortillas, wrap and eat!

Greek Roll Ups

Combine the following ingredients in a bowl:

2 C white beans
1 ½ C diced cucumber
1 C diced tomatoes
⅓ C diced red onion
½ C olives, chopped
2 T lemon juice
1 ½ t oregano
½ t salt
dash pepper

Place lettuce leaves on top of flat tortilla. Spoon filling into middle.

6 corn tortillas
6 lettuce leaves

Roll tortillas into an ice-cream cone shape and enjoy!

Indian Dahl with Spinach

Soak lentils for 20 minutes*. Chop onion and spinach.

Bring water to a boil. Add lentils and seasonings. Simmer for 15 minutes (begin sautéing onion mixture below):

  3 ½ C water

  1 ½ C red lentils
  2 t salt or to taste
  ½ t ground turmeric
  ½ t chili powder

Sauté the following until onions are soft, then add to lentils:

  2 T oil
  1 onion, chopped
  1 t ground cumin
  1 t mustard seed
  1 ½ t garam masala

Add spinach to lentils and simmer for 1 more minute.

  1 lb. spinach, chopped

Stir in milk toward the end of cooking time:

  ½ C coconut milk or thick cashew milk**

Serve hot with rice or as is.

* Lentils can be soaking while chopping spinach and onion. If in a hurry, skip the soaking and simmer a little extra.

** Many coconut milks contain sulfites. For an alternative, blend approximately 1 part cashews and 1 part water.

Mediterranean Lentils

Begin cooking brown rice and lentils. (Allow around an hour for brown rice, or if pressed for time, white rice cooks in 20 minutes.)

Sauté until translucent:

> 3 T olive oil
> 1 C yellow onion, diced
> 1 clove garlic, pressed
> 1 C zucchini, diced

Add the following and simmer until heated thoroughly:

> 1 14.5 oz. can diced tomatoes
> 2 T black olives, diced
> 1 lb. lentils, cooked*
> ½ t basil
> 1 ½ T parsley, chopped
> 1 T lemon juice
> 1 t salt or to taste**

Serve over rice:

> 3 C brown rice, cooked***

*Weight before cooking.

**If lentils were not salted, add more salt to taste.

***Measured after cooking.

Navy Bean Soup

Soak beans overnight. Rinse and drain.

Add the following to pressure cooker or slow cooker:

    1 lb. dried navy beans
    4 C vegetable broth or water
    4 C diced tomatoes
    1 C chopped onion
    1 t paprika
    1 bay leaf
    1 T garlic powder
    ½ t thyme
    1 T salt
    dash pepper
    water enough to cover by an inch

Pressure cook for 10 minutes or in crock pot for 4 hours, until beans are tender.

Serve with a big salad*.

*Try a cucumber salad, tomato salad, or garden salad. See page 66, 63, or 46.

Green Bean Stir Fry

Marinate Tofu: Whisk together the following:

> 4 t salt
> 1 T lemon juice
> 2 T grape juice (optional)*
> 2 t tapioca powder**

Add tofu cubes and set aside to marinate (soak up the flavor of the sauce):

> 10 oz. firm tofu, drained and diced

Boil or steam green beans for about 3 minutes, until bright green and almost tender. Drain and set aside.

> 1 ⅓ lb. green beans, trimmed and halved***

Meanwhile, sauté the following on medium-high heat for 3 to 5 minutes:

> 3 T olive oil
> 6 thin slices ginger root
> 2 medium red onions, halved and thinly sliced
> *tofu (from above, save marinade)*

Add the following and simmer for a few minutes until thickened:

> 1 C vegetable broth or water
> ½ t sesame oil
> *marinade, from tofu above*

Add green beans and stir. Remove from heat and stir in cashews:

> ½ C cashews, dry-roasted

Serve immediately over brown rice.

*Or 1 t frozen grape juice concentrate (optional).

**2 t corn starch would also work. Tapioca is preferred for many gluten and MSG sensitive individuals.

***Fresh green beans are the best, but frozen will also work.

Winter Squash Fettuccine

Whoever heard of a squash pasta? Well, don't be afraid to give this one a try. Surprisingly creamy and savory.

Prepare ahead option: Bake acorn squash*.

Prepare pasta according to package directions. Drain and set aside.

 12 ounces rice pasta (fettuccine style if possible)*

In a large saucepan, heat the following ingredients, stirring constantly:

 3 C thick nut milk (2 ½ C water, 1 ¾ C cashews)
 1 ¼ C canned pumpkin
 2 ½ t salt
 ¾ t nutmeg

Add the following and cook until thoroughly warmed:

 2 green onions, chopped
 1 ½ C acorn squash, peeled, cubed and cooked**

Toss sauce with pasta and serve.

*Asian Food stores carry a rice pasta for Pad Thai noodles that can be used, or use your favorite pasta.

**Cut in half, remove seeds, place cut side down in baking dish, add ½ C water and bake at 350 until squash is soft when poked with a fork. (Allow at least half an hour.)

Lentil Salad

Lentils: Sauté in a large pot until softened, about 5 minutes:

    1 T olive oil (extra virgin, optional)
    1 C chopped onion
    ½ C chopped carrots

Add the following and simmer for 30 – 45 minutes (until lentils are tender but not mushy), stirring occasionally:

    2 C vegetable broth or water
    2 C water
    1 C lentils
    2 parsley sprigs
    ¼ t dried thyme
    1 bay leaf
    1 t salt

Drain lentils, saving ¼ C liquid for the dressing.

Dressing: Whisk together the following in a small bowl:

    ¼ C cooking liquid from lentils (above)
    2 T lemon juice
    ¼ t ground mustard seed
    2 T chopped green onion (or use red onion)
    2 T olive oil
    ½ t salt

Add dressing to the drained lentils and refrigerate for 3 hours.

Add parsley and serve on lettuce leaves.

    2 T finely chopped parsley
    Lettuce leaves for serving (optional)

Ratatouille Pasta

Cook pasta according to package directions.

    3 C spiral rice pasta (Tinkyada)

Sauté the bell pepper and onion until onion is translucent, then add eggplant and zucchini and sauté for three more minutes.

    2 T olive oil
    1 C green bell pepper, sliced in thin strips
    1 small onion, chopped

    2 C eggplant, diced
    2 C zucchini, thinly sliced

Add the following plus the rice pasta and warm through:

    1 t salt or to taste
    3 ½ C spaghetti sauce (any flavor)*

Serve with a large salad** and enjoy!

*See note on spaghetti sauce if MSG sensitive (p.129).

**You might try Barbara's Favorite Romaine Salad p.57 or the quick Tossed Salad p. 45.

Veggie Curried Bean Soup

Sauté the following:

>   1 T vegetable oil
>   1 medium onion
>   2 cloves garlic, pressed
>   1 C red bell pepper, chopped

Puree in a blender:

>   2 16 oz. cans white beans
>   2 ½ C water
>   *sautéed veggies from above*
>   1 t curry paste*
>   1 T lemon juice
>   1 t honey
>   1 ½ t salt or to taste

Heat until warmed through. Serve with a big spinach salad and corn chips.

*See Red Curry Paste recipe p. 121 or use your favorite.

Homemade Tortillas

I learned how to make tortillas from a woman in Costa Rica. They do take some time, so keep the other items simple. They are worth the time when you taste them.

Put the following in a large bowl:

   2 ½ C Masa flour*

Blend in Vita-Mix or blender:

   ½ onion
   3 cloves garlic
   1 C water
   1 t salt

Add blender mixture to Masa flour and stir. Add more water or flour if needed to make a stiff dough. Form into balls (roughly ½ C of dough) and place between two oiled layers of baking sheets and press with back of plate or other flat object. Flatten until thin like packaged corn tortillas. If dough is sticking, try adding a little more flour. If dough is crumbly, add a little more water.

Lightly brown each side on med-high in oiled fry pan. Place tortilla on plate and add the following for tacos:

   beans**, lettuce, fresh spinach, chopped tomatoes
   Optional: salsa (p. 61), or ranch dressing (p.47)

Makes a tastier than normal taco. Or use with dips, salsa, or with soups.

Variation: Add avocados, onions, and/or olives to the homemade tortilla tacos if desired. Also try chopped cucumber, chopped bell peppers, or your favorite veggie.

*Masa flour is just corn flour ground very fine and used in Mexican cooking to make tortillas, tamales and other foods. Most stores carry Masa flour in the Mexican foods section.

**You can use any beans that are well cooked, soft, with little liquid left. Black beans recipe (p. 114) in this cookbook works well (freeze some ahead), as do refried beans.

Crispy Vegetable Pakoras

Mix dry ingredients in a large bowl, then add water and mix until smooth:

    1 C chickpea flour (garbanzo)
    ½ t ground coriander
    1 ½ t salt
    ½ t ground turmeric
    ½ t chili powder
    ½ t garam masala
    2 cloves garlic, crushed

    ¾ C water

Preheat oven to 400. Coat cauliflower and onions in batter.

    ½ head cauliflower florets
    2 onions, sliced into rings

Place on oiled* cookie sheet and bake at 400 degrees for 25 minutes.

Variation: deep fry in 1 quart oil at 375 degrees for 4 to 5 minutes or until brown.

*I prefer olive oil.

Vermicelli 'n' Veggies with Garlic Sauce

Boil water for vermicelli (while water heats, chop the veggies).

Green bean thread vermicelli, 1 bundle

Toss vermicelli in boiling water and turn off heat. Let sit for 3 minutes until soft. Drain and set aside.

Heat oil in skillet over medium heat. Stir fry parsley and garlic in oil until garlic is lightly golden.

¼ C olive oil
¼ C parsley, chopped
6 cloves garlic, minced

Add veggies and cook for roughly three minutes, until veggies are just barely starting to cook.

6 C vegetables*, chopped
salt to taste, maybe 1-2 t (add after veggies are cooked)

This might be nice with a lovely salad and some Ranch Dressing**!

*Try broccoli, red or green bell pepper, onions, celery, and/or carrots. Or create your own combination.
**See Garden Salad p. 46, and Ranch Dressing p. 47.

Broccoli Tomato Quiche

This is a delicious broccoli quiche with a unique potato crust. Start boiling the potato right away, then smash with a fork when it's well done. Or use mashed potatoes if you have some on hand.

Blend in Vita-Mix or blender until smooth:

    ¼ C nuts*
    2 C tofu, firm
    1 T lemon juice
    1 T honey
    2 cloves garlic
    2 t basil
    1 t salt

Pour the mixture into a bowl and stir in the following:

    2 C broccoli, chopped
    1 C tomatoes, chopped

Now that the filling is ready, let's make the crust. Mix the following together:

    ⅓ C mashed potato (a little less than one boiled potato)
    1 C rice flour
    ½ C nut milk**
    1 t salt

Press dough into small baking dish forming a pie crust. Add the filling and bake at 350 for 50 to 60 minutes.

*Cashews, sunflower seeds or pine nuts would work well.

** Use any milk you have on hand or blend ½ C water with ¼ C nuts.

Veggie Taco Casserole

Place corn chips in a 2-quart casserole dish:

    2 C broken corn chips

Mix beans and salsa together and spread on top of corn chips.

    2 16 oz. cans pinto beans with liquid
    1 C salsa (p. 61 or store bought)

Sour Cream: Blend until smooth and spread over beans:

    1 ½ C raw sunflower seeds
    1 ½ C water
    6 T lemon juice
    ¾ t onion powder
    1 ½ t salt

Add the following for the next layer:

    4 green onions, chopped
    2 tomatoes, chopped

Cheesy Sauce: Blend until smooth and pour over the top of the casserole:

    1 C cashews
    3 T pine nuts
    ½ Roma tomato
    ½ t onion powder
    ½ t garlic powder
    1 ½ t salt
    water (just a little as needed to blend)

Bake at 375 until warmed through, about ½ hour. Serve with guacamole and salad.

Lentils with Rosemary and Sage

Cook all ingredients in a slow cooker, on the stove, or in a pressure cooker:

    7 C water
    1 lb. dried lentils
    2 C canned white beans, drained
    3 C onion, chopped
    1 C carrot, diced
    4 cloves garlic, pressed
    1 ½ t dried rosemary, crushed
    1 t sage
    1 bay leaf
    2 t salt

Cooking times:

    Slow cooker: 6 hours on low, 3 hours on high.
    Pot on stove: 45 – 60 minutes.
    Pressure cooker: 12 minutes on high.

Veggie Picadillo

Sauté the tofu, onion, garlic and salt until tofu is lightly browned. Then add the remaining ingredients and sauté for an additional 2 minutes:

    1 T olive oil
    16 oz. crumbled tofu
    1 large onion, chopped
    1 clove garlic, minced
    1 t salt

    1 red bell pepper, chopped
    1 large carrot, finely chopped

Mix in the following and simmer for 15 minutes, stirring occasionally:

    1 C oatmeal*
    ⅓ C raisins
    ½ C water
    ⅛ C green olives, sliced
    1 T lemon juice
    1 bay leaf
    2 Roma tomatoes, chopped
    4 T tomato paste
    1 t salt

Side dish ideas: fresh tomatoes, corn on the cob, or steamed kale.

*See p. 2 for information about celiac disease and oats. Omit if sensitive.

Garlic Mashed Potatoes

Boil the following together in a pot of water:

  6 large baking potatoes
  12 large cloves garlic
  1 bay leaf
  1 T salt

Drain and remove bay leaf (save ¼ C of liquid).

Mash briefly with beaters. Add the following and beat until fluffy:

  ¼ C liquid (from above)
  2 T olive oil
  1 ½ t salt

Serve piping hot and enjoy!

Quick Three Bean Soup

Make beans ahead or just buy canned beans.

Sauté onion and garlic in a saucepan until tender:

    2 T olive oil
    2 onions, chopped
    4 cloves garlic, chopped or pressed

Add remaining ingredients and simmer for 5 minutes:

    4 C white beans
    4 C kidney beans
    4 C black beans
    1-2 C water
    4 C diced tomatoes*
    1 ½ t thyme
    salt to taste

Serve warm. Side dish ideas: crackers and a fruit salad, or fruit plate.

*Or two 14.5 oz cans. MSG sensitive may watch for citric acid or use fresh tomatoes.

Mexican Veggie Stir-Fry

Sauté the following for 4 minutes:

> 2 T olive oil
> 1 t ground cumin
> 1 t dried oregano leaves
> 1 clove garlic, minced
> 1 medium red bell pepper, thinly sliced
> 1 medium onion, cut in thin wedges
> 1 jalapeño pepper, minced*

Then add the following and sauté another 4 minutes:

> 1 ½ lbs. mixed vegetables, fresh or frozen

Add salt at the end:

> ½ t salt

Serving ideas: brown rice and pinto beans with salsa**.

*Deseed to reduce heat, or leave some seeds in if you like it hot.
**Page 61 or your favorite.

Linguine with Zucchini

Bring sauce to a simmer, add pasta and cook until pasta is tender:

    12 oz. pad Thai noodles, soaked for 3 minutes*
    3 C spaghetti sauce

Sauté the following until zucchini is almost tender:

    2 T olive oil
    3 medium zucchini, thinly sliced
    1 ½ medium onions, chopped
    3 cloves garlic, minced
    ¾ t basil
    ¾ t salt

Add sautéed vegetables to the noodles and sauce.

Serve with salad and carrot sticks.

*The noodles used in this recipe are the dry Pad Thai noodles that cook very quickly (3 min. in hot water). If using other linguine style noodles, cook according to package directions, *before* adding to the sauce.

Fragrant Spicy Rice

Start rice right away if using brown rice. Leave alone to simmer while preparing the rest. It's easier than it looks.

Rice: Simmer the following in a pot for 45 minutes* while preparing lentils:

> 2 ½ C vegetable broth (or water)
> 2 green onions, chopped
> 1 t salt
> ⅛ t garam masala**
> ⅛ t turmeric powder
> pinch cayenne pepper
> 1 C uncooked brown Basmati rice*

Lentils and Veggies: In a deep frying pan, sauté the following until garlic starts to brown:

> 2 T olive oil
> 10 large fresh mushrooms
> 5 cloves garlic, chopped

Add the following and simmer for 20 minutes, stirring occasionally:

> ½ green bell pepper, chopped
> ½ red bell pepper, chopped
> 1 C frozen green peas
> ½ C dry red lentils
> ¾ C vegetable broth
> 1 t garam masala**
> pinch turmeric powder
> cayenne pepper to taste

COMBINE sautéed lentil-veggie mixture and rice together. Cook and stir until all the liquid has evaporated. Top with sliced almonds and cilantro if desired.

*If in a hurry, use white Basmati rice and reduce simmering time to 20 minutes.

**If you don't have this Indian seasoning, use a dash each of cinnamon, coriander, and cumin.

Eggplant Curry (Baingan Bharta)

Bake eggplant at 450 degrees for 20 to 30 minutes on a baking sheet:

    1 ½ large eggplant

Sauté the following until onion is tender:

    3 T olive oil
    1 ½ t cumin seeds
    1 ½ medium onion
    2 T garlic, pressed
    1 T ginger root, minced

Add the following and cook for 10 minutes:

    1 ½ T curry paste
    1 ½ tomato, chopped
    ½ C cashews (blended with ½ C water)*
    1 ½ jalapeño chili, deseeded and chopped
    eggplant, chopped, from above
    2 – 3 t salt

Garnish with cilantro and serve

    ½ bunch cilantro, finely chopped

*Or use ¾ C of your favorite milk.

Lasagna Pie

Noodles: Boil the following:

    6 lasagna noodles

Filling: Sauté until tender:

    1 T olive oil
    1 C green bell pepper, chopped
    1 C onion, chopped
    1 12 oz. package firm tofu, drained and crumbled
    3 cloves garlic, pressed
    1 C mushrooms, optional

Add the following and simmer for 10 minutes:

    3 T tomato paste
    1 t Italian seasoning
    1 t fennel seeds
    ¼ t crushed red pepper flakes
    1 25 oz. jar spaghetti sauce
    ½ t salt

Arrange noodles in spoke-like pattern in a lightly oiled 8-inch pie pan, allowing ends to hang over sides. Spread 3 C of the filling over the noodles. Fold the ends of noodles over filling and top with remaining filling and cheesy sauce below. Bake for 20 minutes.

Cheesy Sauce: Blend until smooth and pour over the top of the casserole:

    1 C cashews
    3 T pine nuts
    ½ Roma tomato
    ½ t onion powder
    ½ t garlic powder
    1 ½ t salt
    water (just a little as needed to blend)

Navy Beans with Herb Dumplings

Dumplings: Mix the dry ingredients in a bowl, then blend cashews and water and stir into dry ingredients:

1 ¾ C quinoa flour
1 T garbanzo flour
1 T baking powder
½ t salt
¼ t oregano
¼ t basil

¾ C water
1 C cashews

Veggies and beans: Sauté the following in a deep skillet or Dutch oven for a few minutes:

1 T vegetable oil
12 oz. tofu, crumbled
2 cloves garlic, chopped
1 medium onion, chopped
1 medium stalk celery, chopped
1 t oregano
½ t basil

Add the following and bring to a simmer:

1 16 oz. can navy beans
4 Roma tomatoes, chopped (approximately 2 C)
1 ½ t salt
3 C water

Drop dumplings by spoonfuls on top of the veggies and bean mixture. Simmer on low, uncovered, for 10 minutes. Then cover for another 10 minutes.

Lentil Soup

Simmer the following on the stove for 45 minutes or until lentils are soft:

2 C dry lentils
2 C water
2 potatoes
1 can tomato paste (6 oz)
1 large onion, chopped (reserve ½ C for below)
2 large carrots, chopped (reserve ½ C for below)
2 stalks celery, chopped (reserve ½ C for below)

Blend in Vita-Mix or blender:

1 C water
4 cloves garlic
1 T salt
¼ t rosemary
¼ t thyme
½ C each of the onions, carrots and celery (reserved above)

Add blender mix to lentil soup and heat through.

Suggestion: Serve warm with biscuits, or crackers, and a large green leafy salad. Try red leaf lettuce with tomatoes and sunflower seeds. Squeeze a lemon over the salad and/or use salad dressing.

Tomato Herb Lentil Loaf

This loaf is really good! Try serving with Cashew Gravy drizzled over the top.

Cook lentils and rice ahead*. Mix all ingredients together in a large bowl.

1 C cooked brown lentils
½ C cooked brown rice
½ C ground sunflower seeds
½ C tomatoes, chopped
⅓ C onion, finely chopped
⅓ C celery, finely chopped
5 T tomato paste (½ of a 6 oz. can of tomato paste)
2 t salt
⅛ t sage
1 t garlic powder
½ t onion powder
dash thyme
dash rosemary
dash cayenne (careful, not too much!)
dash basil

Press into an oiled 4" by 8" loaf pan. Bake at 350 for 40 minutes or until brown. Allow to cool in pan. Decorate a serving platter with lettuce leaves and place loaf in middle. Or place directly on serving platter and drizzle cashew gravy over the top.

This is nice at Thanksgiving or during winter.

*Can be cooked ahead and frozen.

Chicken Style Seasoning

Make your own chicken style seasoning using some of the common seasonings. Try this one first and modify as you wish.

    ¼ C salt
    2 T celery salt
    2 T onion powder
    2 T parsley flakes
    2 t turmeric
    1 t garlic
    ¼ t marjoram

Mix well. Store in an airtight container. Use in any recipe calling for chicken seasoning.

Variation: Also try adding some or all of the following as desired:

    ¼ t thyme
    ¼ t rosemary
    ⅛ t oregano
    ¼ t savory
    increase garlic to 2 t or to 1 T

Note: Chicken seasoning nearly always contains MSG. Even when the package says, "No MSG Added" there is still a *high* danger of MSG. "No MSG added" means that they didn't take a bottle of MSG and "*add*" it. MSG can still be present because it is *formed* during the soaking and fermenting process.

Taco Seasoning

¼ C chili powder
2 T ground cumin
1 T oregano
1 t paprika
2 T garlic powder
½ C onion powder
2 T salt

Combine all ingredients and store in a cool, dry place.

Nut Creams

Almond Cream

Very good for dipping fruit.

  2 C soaked almonds
  4 Medjool dates
  2 inches vanilla bean (or 2 t vanilla extract)
  2 C COLD water

Blend in Vita-Mix until smooth. If thick add 1 T water at a time.

Variation: Some people remove the skins from the soaked almonds. Tastes richer, less bitter, and the cream has a whiter look. Even though the soaking helps loosen skins, it can still be quite time-consuming.

Almond Coconut Cream

The coconut is really nice in this!

Blend well in Vita-Mix:

> 2 C almonds (soaked)
> Coconut meat from one coconut
> 3" vanilla bean or 3 t vanilla extract
> 4 Medjool dates
> Cold water, enough to blend

Then add banana and blend until smooth:

> 1 banana (preferably frozen)

Use as a topping, or dip for fruit, or on desserts.

Macadamia Almond Cream

¾ C macadamia nuts, soaked*
½ C almonds, soaked*
¾ C cashews, soaked*
4 Medjool dates
2" vanilla bean or 2 t vanilla extract
1 ¾ C cold water **

Blend in Vita-Mix until smooth. If thick add 1 T water at a time.

*If you don't have time for soaking, just use a little less nuts and a little more water.

**Toss in a couple ice cubes to make it cold.

Cashew Almond Whipped Cream

This makes a whiter colored cream than some others.

Put all ingredients in Vita-Mix and blend until smooth and fluffy. Try to keep it as thick as possible while thinning it with just enough water to blend smoothly. Add more nuts if it gets too thin.

½ C cashews
¾ C slivered blanched almonds
¾ to 1 C cold water*
1 T honey
1" vanilla bean or 1 t vanilla extract

Makes 1 ½ to 2 C whipped cream.

*Toss in some ice cubes to cool.

Cashew Macadamia Whipped Cream

A rich, light, flavorful cream.

    1 ½ C cashews, soaked 1 hour
    ½ C macadamia nuts, soaked 1 hour
    4 Medjool dates
    2 inches vanilla bean or 2 t vanilla extract
    1 ½ C cold water

Blend in Vita-Mix or blender until smooth. If thick, add water, 1 T at a time.

Cashew Banana Whipped Cream

Blend the following ingredients until smooth:

    1 C cashews, soaked 1 hour
    ½ C macadamia nuts or meat from one coconut, optional
    3 Medjool dates
    ½ banana
    3 inches vanilla bean or 3 t vanilla extract
    1 C water (cold)

Near end of blending add:

    ¼ C cashews, soaked 1 hour

Delicious on strawberries, blueberries, peaches...

Note: Use right away or the banana makes it turn a brownish color. If wanting to save some for later use, try adding the juice of an orange, because the citrus will help keep it from turning brown.

Desserts

Chocolate Fudge

A very tasty treat!

Blend until smooth in Vita-Mix or blender:

>   2 C cashews
>   6" vanilla bean*
>   1 C cacao nibs or 6 T cocoa powder
>   2 T liquid lecithin, optional
>   ⅜ C honey

This is very thick so you may need to scrape down the sides. Add 1 to 2 T or more of water if needed.

Spread in a flat container and refrigerate until firm.

*Equals 2 T vanilla extract.

Pumpkin Pie

Makes 2 pies.

Prepare pie crusts ahead of time (see the following recipe).

Preheat oven to 375.

Blend the following until smooth:

> 1 ⅔ C water
> Cashews to bring water
>   level up to 3 C line
> ¼ C Minute tapioca (dry)
> ½ t salt
> ¼ t nutmeg
> ¼ t cloves
> ½ t cinnamon
> dash ginger
> 1 C honey

Add the pumpkin and mix everything together in a bowl:

> Pumpkin, large (29 oz. can)

Pour into unbaked pie crusts and cover with aluminum foil. Bake covered at 375 for 40 minutes, then uncover and bake for 10 more minutes.

Serve warm or cold with your favorite cream if desired. We recommend Cashew Almond Whipped Cream (p. 172) for it's light color and mild flavor.

Pie Crust

These will be heavier than white flour crusts*. Makes 2 pie crusts.

Whiz in blender or Vita-Mix:

> 1 C cashews (soaked**)
> ½ C pecans (soaked**)
> ½ C water
> 1 ½ t salt

Pour into bowl and add rice flour.

> 1 ½ C rice flour (brown or white)

If sticky, add more rice flour. If too crumbly, add more water. Sprinkle a little flour into the pie pan and press the dough into pan to form the crust***.

No prebaking needed for Pumpkin pie and several other pies. For recipes requiring prebaked crusts, bake at 375 for 15 minutes.

*Those who can eat wheat may prefer their regular pie crust.

**If nuts are not soaked, use a little less nuts and a little more water.

***This crust breaks and crumbles when rolled out, so it's easiest to press it into the sides of the pie pan.

Basic Pie Crust

These will be heavier than regular white flour crusts.

Mix the following ingredients:

¾ C rice flour
⅓ C almond or cashew butter
½ t salt

Add water and mix well.

¼ C water

Press into ungreased pie pan. Prick with a fork and bake at 350 until lightly browned.

Works well for both sweet and savory fillings. Makes one bottom crust.

Apple Raisin Pie

Prepare a pie crust first. See p. 179 or any pie crust recipe you like.

Put raisins and water on stove and cook until raisins are plump. Blend *half* of raisins and all the water in Vita-Mix or blender.

    1 ½ C raisins
    ¾ C water

Mix *all* ingredients together (including the blended raisins, whole raisins and the following).

    6-7 sliced apples
    ¼ t cinnamon
    ¼ t nutmeg

Pour into a 9 inch pie crust. Bake in oven at 350 until apples are cooked through (an hour or so). Cover crust with foil when brown to keep from burning.

Blueberry and Cream Delight

Sweet blueberry puree with cream!

Blend the following in Vita-Mix or
blender until smooth:

    1 C almonds, soaked
    2 Medjool dates
    1 ½ inch vanilla bean*
    1 C water
    ½ frozen banana**

Pour equal amounts into 4 goblets or
glasses. Then blend the following in
Vita-Mix or blender until smooth:

    1 frozen banana
    2 Medjool dates
    ¾ to 1 quart blueberries, frozen
    ½ C water***

Pour on top of almond cream in goblets or glasses.

Experiment with different kinds of layering if you'd like! More layers are more work,
but more beautiful and fun.

*Equals 1 ½ t pure vanilla extract

**If banana is not frozen, use some ice cubes in the water.

***You may need to use 1 C water or more if not using a Vita-Mix.

Oatmeal Raisin Cookies

Soak ¾ C raisins in hot water 10 minutes (then drain).

Blend the following items in Vita-Mix or blender:

½ C honey
1 T molasses
½ C oil
3 inches vanilla bean or 1 T vanilla extract
1 t salt
¼ C almonds
½ C water

Mix in another bowl:

¾ C chopped nuts
¾ C soaked raisins (drained)
2 ½ C quick oats*
½ C oat flour or rice flour
1 T tapioca flour

Combine dry ingredients and liquid ingredients. Drop by 2 T portions onto oiled cookie sheet. Bake at 350 for 25 minutes.

*See p. 2 for information about celiac disease and oats.

Blueberry "Milkshake"

A delicious, thick shake that tastes like an old-fashioned blueberry milkshake.

Blend the following in Vita-Mix or blender until smooth:

> 1 C almonds, soaked
> 4 Medjool dates
> 1 ½ inch vanilla bean*
> 1 ½ C cold water**

Add the following and blend again:

> 1 or 2 frozen bananas
> ¾ to 1 quart blueberries, frozen

Enjoy!

*Equals 1 ½ t pure vanilla extract.
**Put some ice cubes in the water to cool.

Coconut Peach "Ice Cream"

Blend in Vita-Mix until smooth:

> ¼ C pecans
> 1 C cold water
> 1 T honey

Add the following and blend until it looks like soft ice-cream:

> ⅓ frozen banana
> 1 ½ C frozen peaches
> ½ C coconut milk or meat from ½ coconut (frozen if possible)

Top with strawberries or raspberries!

Note: Coconut meat can be frozen in a zip-lock bag or coconut milk can be frozen in ice-cube trays. If coconut was not frozen, just make the water and other items really cold.

Chocolate "Ice Cream"

Tastes like old-fashioned homemade ice-cream. Make nut milk ahead and freeze in ice-cube tray.

Blend the following in Vita-Mix until smooth and freeze to make nut milk cubes:

¼ C nuts (almond, pecan, cashew)
½ C dried coconut
4 C water
3 T honey
1 t vanilla

When the cubes are frozen, blend the following until smooth:

¼ C pecans
¼ C coconut, dried, shredded
1 C water
4 T honey
2 T cocoa powder
½ t vanilla

Add approx. 18 frozen nut milk cubes (4 C). Blend for 30-90 seconds just until smooth.

Banana Bread Brownies

Preheat oven to 375.

Blend in Vita-Mix or blender until smooth:

> 1 ripe banana
> ¼ C oil
> ¾ C honey
> ½ C water
> 1 T chopped almonds
> ¼ t almond extract or ½ t vanilla

Mix the following together in a large bowl:

> 1 ⅜ C quinoa flour
> ½ t baking powder
> ½ t baking soda
> ½ t salt

Add the wet ingredients to the bowl then add:

> ½ C coconut fat* (skimmed off top of can) or oil

Stir well. Then fold in the nuts:

> ½ C chopped walnuts

Pour into oiled 9x9 cake pan and bake for 20 minutes or until toothpick comes out clean.

*Note: When a can of coconut milk is cold, the fat rises to the top. Simply scoop off the thick fat. If coconut milk is not separating, use more coconut milk and add less water. Coconut fat is nicer, but you can also replace it with any cooking oil (I like extra light olive oil).

Chocolate Coconut Brownies

Soft, fluffy cakes that anyone will eat.

Mix the following ingredients together:

> 1 ¼ C quinoa flour
> ¼ C cocoa powder
> ½ t baking powder
> ½ t baking soda
> ½ t salt

In a separate bowl, stir the following together:

> ⅜ C oil
> ¼ C water
> ¾ C honey
> ¼ t almond extract
> ½ C coconut milk fat (off top of can)*

Pour wet mixture into dry mixture and stir until well mixed.

Pour into oiled pan or muffin tins and bake at 375 for 17 minutes.

Makes a 9 x 13 pan or a dozen muffins.

*MSG/sulfite sensitive individuals may need to watch for sulfites (metabisulfite, or anything ending in sulfite) and anything extract. You could substitute a thick nut cream. Just blend 1 part cashews and roughly 1 part water (enough to make it thick). Use this instead of coconut fat.

Applesauce Cookies

Mix the following:

> 3 C rolled oats*
> 1 ¼ C brown rice flour
> ¼ t sea salt
> ⅓ C chopped Medjool dates or raisins
> ⅓ C chopped pecans

Stir in:

> 1 C applesauce
> ¾ C oil
> 1 t vanilla
> ¾ C honey

Form into cookie shapes ½ inch thick and place on oiled cookie sheet. Bake for 10 minutes at 350.

Variation: press thumb print into cookies before baking and fill with jelly after they cool.

*Celiac individuals may need to avoid oats (see p. 2). Others who are gluten intolerant may be able to use oats, so we included this recipe.

Bananas in Coconut Milk

Desert treat from Thailand!

Heat the following until it begins to bubble.

   4 C coconut milk
   ¼ C water (omit if using Lite Coconut Milk)
   ½ – ⅔ C honey
   ¼ t salt

Add banana chunks and simmer for two minutes.

   2-3 small, slightly green bananas, sliced in ½" chunks

Serve hot or cold.

Strawberry Dreams Dessert

For this beautifully layered dessert, you will need:

Nut Crumble (below)
Creamy Orange Clouds (below)
4 bananas
2 pints fresh strawberries or more

Nut Crumble

Blend the following in a K-tec Total Blender or a Vita-Mix until mostly fine nut powder:

1 ½ C almonds
¼ t Celtic sea salt
dash cinnamon
dash nutmeg

Add the Following and blend just a few more seconds:

3 Medjool dates
dash olive oil

Finish mixing in the dates by hand if necessary.

Creamy Orange Clouds

Blend the following in a Vita-Mix until smooth:

1 C cashews
juice of 1 small lemon
juice of 1 large orange (or 2 small)
5 Medjool dates

NOTE: If your lemon is large or very sour, you may want to use half. You want just a touch of the sour flavor, but still sweet enough with more orange flavor.

Decoratively Layer this Beautiful Dessert

Crust:

Slice **bananas** directly onto a *large* platter to make a single layer.
Sprinkle **Nut Crumble** in a thin layer to fill in the spaces between bananas.*

Clouds:

Pour half of the **Creamy Orange Clouds** over the Crust**.

Floating Strawberries:

Slice a mountain of fresh strawberries directly onto the orange fluff layer. Use at least two pints***. Pile them HIGH!

---

*The crumble should be fairly light, because the creamy layer already makes this dessert *very* rich.

**Use the other half as a dip for strawberries for breakfast!

***Strawberries are not just for decoration. Piles of juicy strawberries are needed to balance the richness of the nuts. In addition, a HEAPING mound of strawberries makes this dessert SO PRETTY!

Sesame Halva

Put all ingredients through Champion-type juicer using the blank plate:

    8 oz sesame seeds (without hulls) or tahini
    4 oz raisins
    4 oz Medjool dates
    1 t vanilla extract
    Pinch of salt or to taste

Mix together well and press into oiled 9 x 9 pan or roll into balls.

Banana Chocolate Mousse

Very smooth and creamy. Wonderful layered with blueberry smoothie.

Blend until smooth in Vita-Mix or blender:

    8 Medjool dates
    1 C cashews
    6" vanilla bean*
    ½ C cacao nibs or 6 T cocoa powder
    1 banana, fresh or frozen
    1 C water

Serve warm or chilled.

*Equals 2 T vanilla extract.

Chocolate Covered Nuts

It's hard to imagine a tasty chocolate without milk and sugar, but these delicious treats will satisfy the chocolate cravings of the health-minded!

Blend the following until smooth and creamy:

> 4 T cocoa powder
> 8 Medjool dates
> ½ C cashews
> ½ C coconut oil
> 4 inches vanilla bean, or 4 t vanilla extract

Place nuts on plate or tray and pour chocolate mixture over them.

> 1 – 1 ½ C of nuts (choose from almonds, pecans, cashews, macadamia, peanuts, etc.)

Freeze or refrigerate until firm (around 30 minutes in freezer). Keep them cool until eating (coconut oil softens at room temperature).

Chocolate Mousse

Very smooth and creamy. Wonderful layered with a blueberry smoothie.

    8 Medjool dates
    1 C cashews
    6" vanilla
    ½ C cacao nibs or 6 T cocoa powder
    1 C water

Blend until smooth in Vita-Mix or blender. Serve warm or chilled.

Nut Cookies

Quick and easy, no-bake cookies!

Process all ingredients in a food processor or Vita-Mix until smooth. Mixture will be fairly stiff, so you may need to scrape down the sides a few times.

6 C cashews
1 C Brazil nuts
½ C macadamia nuts
meat from ½ a young coconut
8-10 Medjool dates
1 C raisins
1 t cinnamon
2 t salt
1 t flaxseed oil, optional

Roll into small balls. These are very rich so a small cookie is very satisfying.

Drinks

Heavenly Chai

This is such a creamy, creamy drink! Replace your hot chocolate with this version of Heavenly Chai.

    1 C cashews (preferably soaked 1 hour)
    1 C macadamia nuts (preferably soaked 1 hour)
    4 Medjool dates
    2 inches vanilla bean (or 2 t vanilla extract)
    1 inch piece fresh ginger
    ½ t cinnamon
    ¼ t cardamom
    ¼ t ground cloves
    2 ½ C water

Blend in Vita-Mix or blender until smooth (if you are using a regular blender, you may want to strain out any chunks by pouring it through a cheesecloth).

Cranberry Drink

A great holiday drink with a brilliant red color, fabulous at Christmas!

    6 oz cranberries (½ of a 12 oz bag)
    7 Medjool dates
    2 T lemon or lime juice (freshly squeezed)
    3 C water (add a few ice cubes for a cool drink)

Blend in Vita-Mix or blender until smooth. Add more water if needed.

Strawberry Drink

Blend the following in Vita-Mix or blender until smooth:

    1 C almonds, soaked
    2 C strawberries, fresh or frozen
    2 bananas, fresh or frozen
    2 C orange juice, fresh squeezed (3-4 oranges) or 2 C water
    ¼ t nutmeg
    2 inches vanilla bean or 2 t vanilla extract

Makes a delicious breakfast or supper for two or a tasty dessert for 4-6.

Variation 1: Add 1-2 t spirulina or blue-green algae for extra nutrients.

Variation 2: Add 2 T flax oil for omega 3 essential fatty acids.

Raspberry Milk

Put all the ingredients and just half the water in Vita-Mix or blender until smooth.

    2 C raspberries
    $^1/_3$ banana
    3 T pecans
    5 Medjool dates
    2 inches vanilla bean (or 2 t vanilla extract)
    2 C water (start with 1 C)

Add the rest of the water and blend again briefly.

Makes 3 to 4 C of raspberry milk.

Variation: Try strawberries or blueberries instead of the raspberries. For more variety, use almonds, cashews, or macadamia nuts in place of pecans.

Index

For your scribbling pleasure!

Future Inspirational Cookbooks

Ideas for Future cookbooks that may be coming soon!

The Great Smoothie Cookbook with gazillions of recipes you can't wait to try including amazing green smoothies for health and great taste. Get your greens in without knowing it.

Young Thai Coconut Cookbook

Afresh! Adding in some raw food dishes for the average family

Pure and Simple 2nd Edition with more recipes to inspire healthy cooking!

Celiac products

We are developing a line of products to help keep gluten-sensitive and celiac people safe and healthy. Possible products: soaps, toothpaste, gluten free foods and educational materials. We are open to suggestions. **Come to madebyceliacs.com for more information.**

madebyceliacs.com

"Help, I need a Vita-Mix!"

If you've worn out your blender or it's just too slow, it might be time for a Vita-Mix.

Most blenders are 350 watts. The Vita-Mix is 1400 watts. The difference in power is amazing.

If you can find a good deal, snatch it up! If you don't find a sale, we can at least save you shipping. Come to our website! See foodasgrown.com

To order more cookbooks go to foodasgrown.com

Web Sites

http://foodasgrown.com contains more information on health and lifestyle as well as many books, DVDs and other healthful living products.

http://www.drfuhrman.com Dr. Fuhrman wrote *Eat to Live*, an extremely helpful book on health and the power of nutrition.

http://www.paradiseraw.com gives great information on adding in more raw foods to your diet.

http://digestive.niddk.nih.gov/ddiseases/pubs/celiac National Digestive Diseases Information Clearinghouse (NDDIC). Basic facts and symptoms of celiac disease.

http://health.groups.yahoo.com/group/SillyYaks A *great* place to chat and find support for those with celiac disease and gluten intolerance.

http://www.enterolab.com Information about celiac disease, gluten intolerance and antibody testing (screening for gluten sensitivity and autoimmune response to gluten).

http://msgmyth.com has helpful information about avoiding MSG and an MSG free discussion board.

To order more cookbooks go to foodasgrown.com

"The China Study" Author Speaks Live in Walla Walla

Powerful evidence in favor of a vegan diet. If you liked the book, this video is a GREAT compliment to it. See and hear the author himself sharing his personal journey and discoveries. If you haven't read it yet, or you got stuck in the middle of the book, this video will make it easier and wet your appetite for more.

The China Study, a national bestselling book, reveals the **world's most comprehensive study of nutrition ever conducted**. In this 3 DVD set, Dr. Campbell explains what he learned from this and many other studies. Surprising evidence piled up study after study pointing out the biggest cause of cancer. He shares how he changed his own life as a result of what he learned.

World famous researcher, Dr. T. Colin Campbell reveals practical hints to avoid cancer, heart disease, diabetes and other diseases. Don't get swept away with unsupported theories. Find scientific facts from the world's top nutrition researcher. Share it with your loved ones and friends.

This 3 DVD set is the most comprehensive video set of Dr. Campbell available anywhere. Over 4 1/2 hours of powerful information, including three presentations with question and answer sessions.

> **Discover how to:**
> **Lose weight**
> **Prevent cancer**
> **Avoid diabetes**
> **Reverse heart disease**

This information can help you avoid cancer which could save you significantly in medical costs. Avoid one trip to the doctor and you may have covered the price of the videos.

Simplified way to gain the highlights of over 40 years of research. You don't even have to read a book, if you don't want. Just grab some popcorn and your favorite chair and watch! In three sessions, you will have solid facts to take charge of your health. **Available at foodasgrown.com**